available at

Editor's Picks

Betrayal
ALEATHA ROMING

"Wow! I was so looking forward to reading this, I love Aleatha's writing and Betrayal didn't disappoint!"

– Sarah T,

Paperback: £12.20

https://amzn.to/4fbN1pM

Faith
MIMI BARBOUR

"Was so glad to have Faith's story. Read first 4 books in the series and having Faith with her own happy ending, after all she had been through, was icing on the cake."

– Fran Kershner

Kindle: £0.85

https://amzn.to/3YwVY7p

Beautiful and Terrible Things
S.M. STEVENS

a compelling literary novel with resonant themes and characters that stay with readers after the last page is turned.

– Readers' Favorite

Paperback: £22.46

https://amzn.to/46hTQ53

The Hidden Gospel of Thomas
WILLIAM G. DUFFY

"I found new dimensions of Spirituality in reading this book, which is dear to my heart."

– Margaret Earing,

Paperback £12.99

https://amzn.to/3SjkhSb

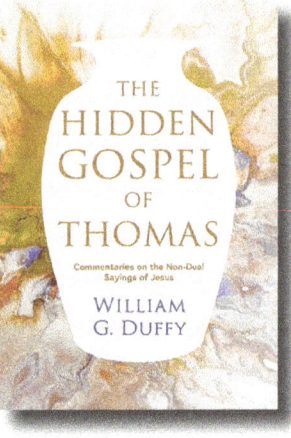

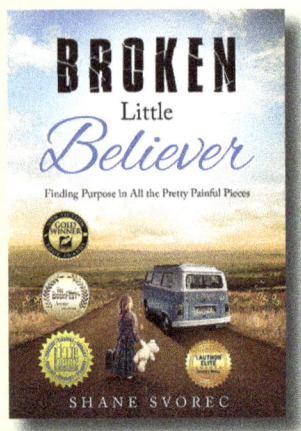

Broken Little Believer
SHANE SVOREC

"Wow, I could not put this book down! Shane is a talented writer and a beacon of light to all who have faced adversity and struggled to find their way. She gives each of us hope and inspiration that through faith, determination, and a positive attitude, there is a rainbow at the end of the storm. Wonderful book!"

–Barbara Kane, lifelong educator,

Hardcove: £12.43

https://amzn.to/4cPQTv7

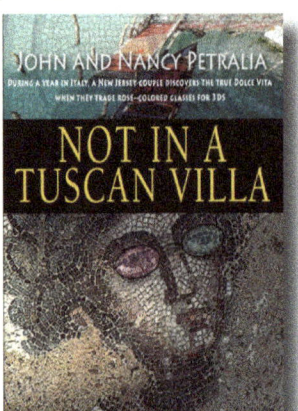

Not In a Tuscan Villa
JOHN AND NANCY PETRALA

I so enjoyed this book that I read it straight through twice! A friend introduced me to it, and it is a very amusing account of a couples year living in Tuscany, but not at all sweet and cloying.

– Barbara Barrettt

Paperback: £11.14

https://amzn.to/4bVJ1GY

She Serves the Realm
LEE SWANSON

"A recommended read for those who like tales of strong women who defy stereotypes, beleaguered kings and nobles, and medieval England."

–J.P. Reedman, author of the Medieval Babes series

Paperback: £15.88

https://amzn.to/3A437By

Independence
CHRISTOPHER C TUBBS

Independence by Christopher C. Tubbs is a thrilling blend of naval warfare, espionage, and historical intrigue. A must-read masterpiece!

–Dan Peters, Reader's House,

paperback: £11.78

https://amzn.to/3zT3qPK

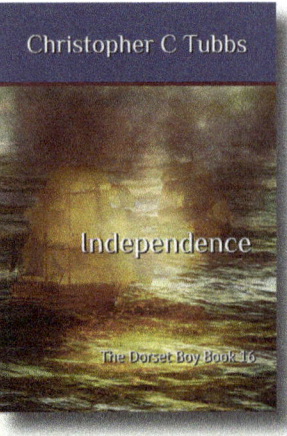

Your Gateway to Endless Stories

Escaping My Demons
JOSEPH FAGARAZZI

"Escaping My Demons is a hard-hitting, riveting, emotional memoir by Joseph Fagarazzi! The book focuses on the turbulent and tense relationships between Joseph and his parents, particularly his selfish, abusive, and exploitative father."

– Steven Setil

Kindle: £7.95

https://amzn.to/3xZ4Mbg

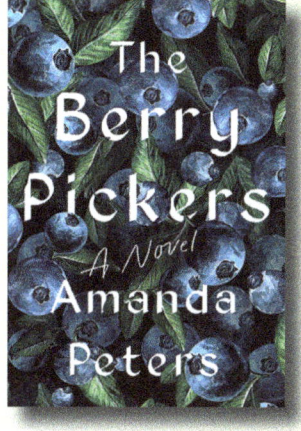

The Berry Pickers
AMANDA PETERS

"A gripping read, a mystery and a moving narrative all in one book."

– A New York Post Best Book of the Year

Paperback: £7.49

https://amzn.to/4bUk2DS

Thirteen Days in Milan
JACK ERICKSON

"The characters and plot in Jack Erickson's *Thirteen Days in Milan* are alive, and the novel has enormous vitality."

– Eduardo Elgani

Paperback: £8.40

https://amzn.to/4f7qD0V

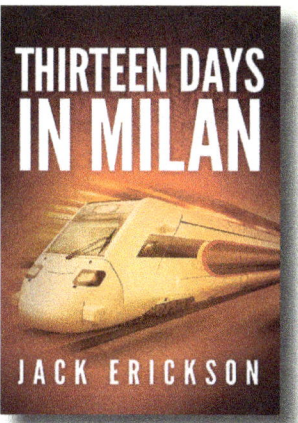

Run with It
JOE DRAKE

"You write beautifully, you've got both a sense of humor and a engineer's ability to make complex biological processes accessible to the non-scientist."

– Amazon Reviewer,

Hardcove: £19.54

https://amzn.to/3Lyt92n

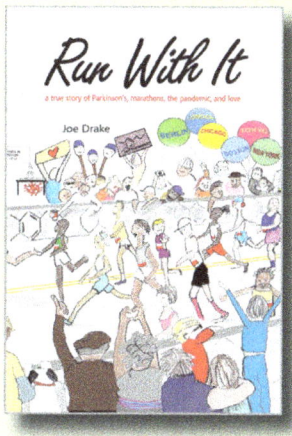

The Lost Bookshop
EVIE WOODS

"The story itself was fascinating. I loved all the details in the story.."

–Sandra A Harvey

Paperback: £8.99

https://amzn.to/3y8sdib

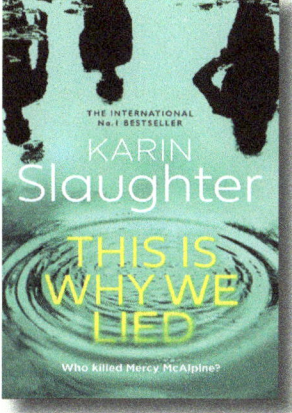

This is Why We Lied
KARIN SLAUGHTER

'Never less than nail-biting'

– The Times

Hardcover: £10.00

https://amzn.to/3zTe4pF

Savage Game
KAREN NAPPA

"About consent, but Karen Nappa, has usual found a way to play with dark desire, empowerment, seduction, and to create truly beautiful true consent. She is a master at this."

–Charnly M.

Paperback: £10.24

https://amzn.to/3WizHqW

A Paper Orchestra
MICHAEL JAMIN

"As one of the head writers for my tv show Maron, Michael Jamin was essential in helping me portray myself honestly. I'm very happy and impressed that he was able to apply his craft to himself..."

– Marc Maron

Hardcover: £20.73

https://amzn.to/3A1DuBn

IN THIS ISSUE

Behind the Books. A Closer Look
In-depth Interviews with Celebrated Authors

TERRY OVERTON p.8	DON HUGHES p.40
MARC POLETT p.10	MALCOLM WELSHMAN p.42
REBECCA VICTOR p.20	ROBERT EMMERS p.44
GLENDA MITCHELL p.22	WAYNE ENGLISH p.46
JOSEPH SEECHACK p.24	JEFF KELLAND p.48
ADEBOLA AJAO p.26	ANNE PENN p.50
BRIAN HATHAWAY p.28	PENNY C. KNIGHT p.52
KM. Taylor p.30	WENDY ZUCCARELLO p.54
R.C. VIELEE p.32	CARINA STEINBAKK p.56
DENISE ALICEA p.34	BETH JORDAN p.58
MICHÈLE OLSON p.36	BOBBI GROOVER p.60
CORDELL PARVIN p.38	

16 to 19
Editor's Choice

10
ON THE COVER

From Jakarta to Bestseller
JESSE SUTANTO
A Journey Through Humour, Mystery, and Family Dynamics

Author Jesse Sutanto discusses her writing journey, inspirations behind Dial A for Aunties, familial themes, cinematic approach, Netflix adaptation, and upcoming releases, offering a glimpse into her captivating world.

SCAN TO READ ONLINE

EDITOR'S LETTER

Welcome to the 46th issue of Reader's House magazine! We are thrilled to bring you another edition filled with literary treasures, insightful interviews, and a celebration of storytelling in all its forms. This issue is particularly special as we feature the remarkable Jesse Sutanto on our cover, a luminary in both children's and adult literature whose works resonate with humour, mystery, and familial depth.

Jesse Sutanto's journey from a crisis-ridden undergrad to a Master's graduate from the University of Oxford is nothing short of inspiring. In an exclusive interview, she shares how she found solace and purpose in creative writing, leading to the creation of her debut novel, *Dial A for Aunties*. This novel, a delightful blend of humour and mystery, is a testament to her ingenuity and personal connection to family dynamics. Jesse's background in film and television production adds a cinematic quality to her storytelling, making her narratives unfold like scenes in a movie. Excitingly, *Dial A for Aunties* has been optioned for adaptation into a Netflix movie, marking a significant milestone in her career.

In addition to our feature on Jesse Sutanto, this issue includes interviews with a stellar line-up of bestselling, award-winning, and exceptional authors. We had the privilege of speaking with Terry Overton, Marc Polett, Rebecca Victor, Glenda Mitchell, Joseph Seechack, Adebola Ajao, Brian Hathaway, Km. Taylor, R.C. Vielee, Denise Alicea, Michèle Olson, Cordell Parvin, Don Hughes, Malcolm Welshman, Robert Emmers, Wayne English, Jeff Kelland, Anne Penn, Penny C. Knight, Wendy Zuccarello, Carina Steinbakk, Beth Jordan, and Bobbi Groover. Each of these authors brings a unique voice and perspective to the literary world, and their insights are sure to inspire and captivate our readers.

Jesse Sutanto's upcoming releases, including the final instalment of the Aunties series, *The Good, The Bad, and The Aunties*, and a dark suspense thriller, *You Will Never Be Me*, promise to push boundaries and offer fresh perspectives. Her dedication to representation and authenticity shines through in her work, leaving an indelible mark on literature.

As we celebrate the achievements of these incredible authors, we hope their stories and insights inspire you to explore new narratives, embrace diverse voices, and find joy in the world of books.

Thank you for being a part of the Reader's House community.

Happy reading!

A, Harlowe

Editor's Desk

PUBLISHER
Reader's House
A Subsidiary of Newyox Media
https://newyox.media

200 Suite
134-146 Curtain Road
EC2A 3AR London
t: +44 79 3847 8420

editor@readershouse.co.uk
readershouse.co.uk

EDITORIAL
A. Harlowe
editor@readershouse.co.uk
Dan Peters
dan.peters@readershouse.co.uk
Ben Alan
ben.alan@readershouse.co.uk

CONTRIBUTORS
Claudine D. Reyes
Acacia Baldie
Andrea Piacquadio
Adrian T. Cheng
Donna Schim
Jon Allo
Tim Halloran
Oleg Magni
Amir SeilSepour
Bill Youngblood
Jetty Stutzman
Jimmy Choo
Peter Filinovich
Rrodnae Productions

Reader's House
readershouse.co.uk

We assume no responsibility for unsolicited manuscripts or art materials provided from our contributors.

PHOTO: *Terry Overton: Retired professor, award-winning author, and storyteller extraordinaire, blending education and faith through the power of storytelling*

From Classroom to Cathedral - The Journey of
TERRY OVERTON
A Retrospective on Education, Faith, and the Power of Storytelling

Terry Overton, retired professor, discusses her transition from academia to Christian fiction, blending teaching, faith, and award-winning storytelling

Embarking on a journey through the corridors of Terry Overton's life and work reveals a profound dedication to education, psychology, and faith. With a repertoire spanning from the realms of academia to the realms of storytelling, Overton's multifaceted career showcases a remarkable blend of expertise and creativity. A retired university professor boasting accolades in educational and school psychology, Overton's contributions to the field have left an indelible mark. Yet, it is her foray into the world of Christian literature that truly illuminates her passion for teaching and storytelling.

From the very foundation of her career, teaching has been the cornerstone of Overton's endeavours. Beginning in the trenches of public schools, she honed her focus on the individual learning needs of children, a principle that would remain steadfast throughout her professional journey. Transitioning to the realm of higher education, she expanded her scope to encompass the provision of educational strategies and psychological insights to aspiring educators and counsellors. As a dean and department chair, her mentorship extended beyond the classroom, nurturing the growth of faculty and administrators alike.

Now, in her role as a Christian author, Overton's commitment to teaching finds new expression. Through a diverse array of literary endeavours, she endeavours to impart Scripture and Christian values to readers of all ages. Whether weaving tales of time travel in the Newton Chronicles or exploring themes of resilience in The Journey: The Underground Book Readers, Overton seamlessly integrates her faith into narratives that captivate and inspire.

In Legends of the Donut Shop, Overton draws from personal experiences and family stories to craft a narrative imbued with themes of second chances, forgiveness, and the transformative power of faith. Inspired by the camaraderie of her late father and his comrades, she breathes life into characters whose journeys mirror her own encounters with faith and redemption.

Balancing the rigors of academic writing with the artistry of storytelling is no small feat, yet Overton navigates this terrain with finesse. Drawing upon her background in educational psychology, she infuses her Christian fiction with a depth of understanding and a commitment to authenticity. Through meticulous research and consultation with theological experts, she ensures that her narratives resonate with readers on both intellectual and spiritual levels.

Overton's literary endeavours have garnered acclaim, with awards such as the Firebird Book Awards and the International Book Award Finalist lending credence to her

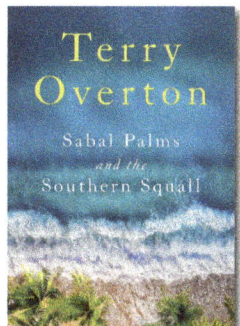  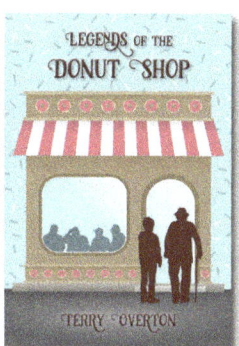 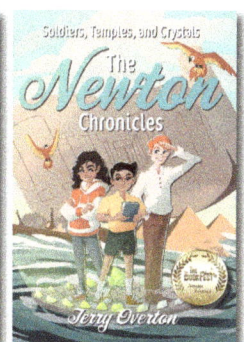 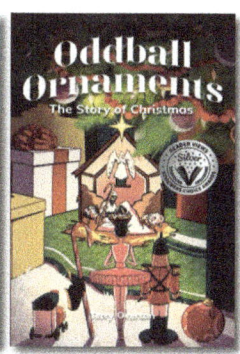

Legends of the Donut Shop: A captivating tale of faith, forgiveness, and second chances, by award-winning author Terry Overton.

work. Yet, beyond the accolades lies a deeper mission—to share the good news and grow the church through the power of storytelling. With each book she pens, Overton seeks to ignite a spark of faith in the hearts of her readers, guiding them on a journey of discovery and transformation.

As she continues to chart new territories in the realm of Christian literature, Overton's unwavering dedication to teaching and storytelling serves as a beacon of inspiration. Through her words, she invites readers to embark on a journey of faith, hope, and endless possibility—a journey that promises to leave an indelible mark on the soul.

Your background in educational and school psychology is extensive, with experience ranging from teaching to serving as a college dean. How has this background influenced your approach to writing Christian books and devotionals?

Teaching has been at the heart of all my professional positions and continues to be the centre of my writing. Teaching in public schools my focus was on individual learning needs of children. Teaching at the university level changed my focus to

Diane M. Dresback, award-winning author, and filmmaker, shares insights into her creative process and storytelling journey in an exclusive interview.

providing sound educational strategies, psychological, and behavioural techniques for teachers, counsellors, and school psychologists. As a university department chair and dean, my focus was mentoring faculty and young administrators. Now, as a Christian author, I strive to teach Scripture and Christian values. This might mean incorporating Bible history into a time travel series (Newton Chronicles), teaching the true meaning of Christmas using animated ornaments (The Oddball Ornaments), or teaching about Heaven and standing up for what is right (Legends of the Donut Shop).

Your book The Journey: The Underground Book Readers explores themes of resilience and perseverance in a dystopian world. What inspired you to write this series, and how do you integrate Christian values into the narrative?

Last year I interviewed school and community librarians about the current attempts to censor classic literature and Christian books in their own libraries and administrative structure. Their testimony inspired me to write a series that would place young readers in a world where books were banned, schools destroyed, and churches burned. The parents of the teen characters had been taken or "disappeared." This left the teens and preteens in a world that would be of their own making. They were determined to continue to read, study, and even have their own church in an underground cavern. The children and teens in the series faced threats at every turn and had to rely on each other and the guidance from God through Scripture for survival.

Legends of the Donut Shop delves into themes of second chances, life lessons, and forgiveness. Can you discuss how your own experiences and beliefs inform the messages conveyed in this book?

This book was inspired by my late father and his buddies, all veterans of the Korean War, WWII, or Vietnam, who met each week at the local donut shop for fellowship and fun. Tales of my father-in-law, and my son-in-law, a rancher in Texas, are also incorporated in the story. The opening scene, a near-death experience, is based on my own near-death experience from thirty years ago. In the story, a teenage boy has a near-death experience and goes back in time to his childhood visits to the donut shop with his grandfather. He hears the same stories he heard before but this time, each story conveys a meaning he now understands. He at last embraces the meaning of Scripture and the Bible he had only superficially absorbed as a child. The same experience of renewed faith happened to me, and to many others who have had near-death experiences. Following this experience, I understood life after death, and I am secure in knowing where I will be following the transition from life to death and Heaven. My dad passed from Covid before he ever read the book. He had seen the cover and three weeks later, he contracted Covid. My mother passed the day before my dad. Dad's buddies from the donut shop were the pallbearers at the funeral. I was blessed to give each on a copy of the book inspired by their group and my dad.

As a retired university professor, you've authored textbooks and journal articles in the fields of special education and school psychology. How do you balance the academic rigor of your professional writing with the storytelling elements of your Christian fiction?

Research was always something I loved about academia. In Christian writing, I conduct similar research on Biblical history, Jewish heritage, world geography, world history, the history of the United States, and historic documents. Authentic Christian fiction requires research. This must be carefully weighed with theological leanings and theological works. When possible, I consult with others who can provide more insight (Rabbis of Jewish faith and heritage, Messianic Jewish Rabbis, Christian pastors, etc.).

Your books have received several awards, including the Firebird Book Awards and the International Book Award Finalist. How do you feel these accolades have impacted your writing career and your mission to share the good news through your books?

It is hard to determine if the awards have much impact on my career, but I do feel receiving awards might bring credibility to my writing. Perhaps parents, teachers, or librarians might be more inclined to read a book that has had an award.

Assessing Learners with Special Needs: An Applied Approach is a practical guide for educators. How do you see your expertise in educational psychology intersecting with your passion for writing Christian fiction and devotionals?

My writing is geared to teaching as it was in the assessment textbook. In the future, I will be offering study guides for some of the Christian books for children.

Polett's Journey Through 'Lily's Wondrous World'

MARC POLETT

Exploring Nature, Friendship, and Imagination in the Pages of Polett's First Literary Endeavour

Marc Polett shares insights into crafting 'Lily's Wondrous World,' drawing from personal experiences and aspirations, inspiring young minds to embrace nature's magic.

Marc Polett, a passionate writer and storyteller, brings his readers into a world where nature's beauty intertwines with childhood wonder in *Lily's Wondrous World: A Day in the Park*. Inspired by his wife's innate connection with animals and his own fond memories of exploring the outdoors, Polett's book encapsulates the essence of adventure and friendship through the eyes of Lily.

Born and raised amidst the scenic landscapes of Gladwyne, PA, Polett's upbringing steeped in nature's embrace laid the groundwork for his creative journey. From capturing moments with deer and rabbits along the trails to immersing himself in the art of storytelling, Polett's childhood experiences set the stage for the enchanting tale of Lily.

With a diverse background spanning from web development to finance, Polett found solace and fulfillment in the art of writing. His journey from scripting poems to crafting narratives reflects a seamless fusion of creativity and expertise honed through various professional endeavors. Through *Lily's Wondrous World*, Polett invites readers to embark on a whimsical journey that celebrates the joys of nature and the magic of companionship.

In a conversation with Reader's House Magazine, Polett delves into the inspirations behind his storytelling, the creative process of blending text and illustrations, and the profound impact of children's literature on nurturing curiosity and empathy. With heartfelt insights and invaluable advice, Polett encourages aspiring writers to embrace their unique narratives and embark on their own creative odysseys.

Lily's Wondrous World not only entertains young readers but also instills timeless values of friendship, exploration, and appreciation for the world around us. Polett's enchanting tale serves as a poignant reminder of the profound impact storytelling holds in shaping the minds and hearts of children, fostering a deep-rooted connection with nature and loved ones alike.

Your book, *Lily's Wondrous World: A Day in the Park*, is inspired by your wife's love of animals and your childhood experiences in nature. Can you share more about how these influences shaped the creation of Lily's adventure?

My wife has always loved

'Lily's Wondrous World: A Day in the Park' by Marc Polett invites readers on a whimsical adventure through nature's wonders.

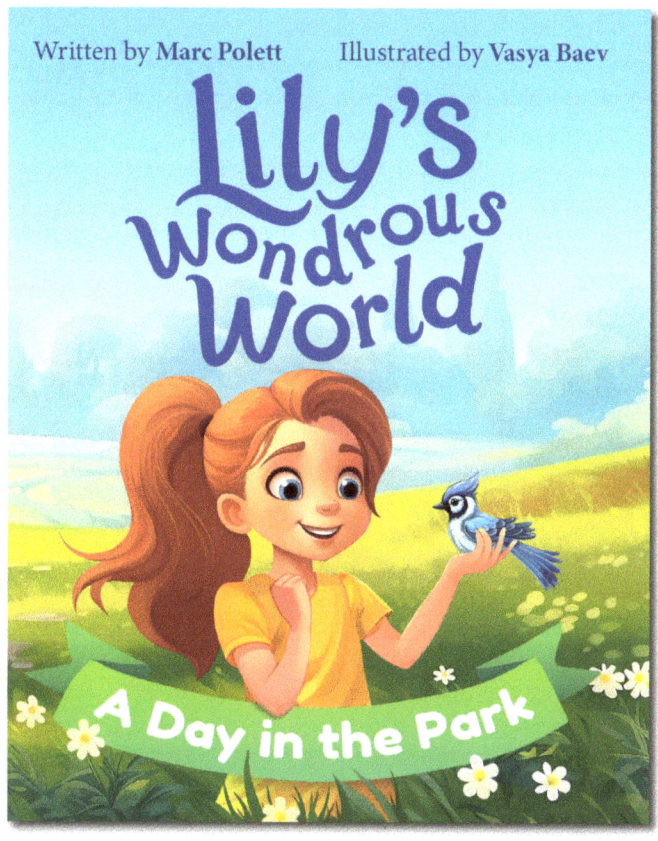

Marc Polett, author of Lily's Wondrous World: A Day in the Park, shares insights into his creative journey and inspirations.

As someone with a background in web development and finance, what drew you to writing and storytelling as your preferred form of creative expression?

Starting from an early age, I've always enjoyed creative writing, and wrote several scripts and poems which were excellent practice for writing in college, graduate school, and the professional world. I majored in Sociology at the University of Arizona, but also studied poetry and creative writing, which helped to hone my skills. I also enjoy graphic arts and coding which is what led me to web and mobile game development. An interest in the stock market and healthcare led me to my career in healthcare finance.

Lily's Wondrous World captures the joy of childhood friendships and the wonders of nature. What message or values do you hope young readers will take away from Lily's adventure?

I hope they'll get excited about the outdoors and exploring nature. There are so many beautiful things to see and wonderful animals that can be found in parks, on trails, or even in one's backyard. I also hope that reading my story inspires others to write their own. Everyone has a story to tell. This is my wife's story and she trusted me to tell it.

The book's poetic narrative and colorful illustrations make it engaging for children aged 4 to 8. How did you approach balancing the text and illustrations to create an immersive reading experience for young readers?

I wrote the story before I found my illustrator. When I met Vasya Baev, we were immediately on the same page for what we wanted to accomplish with this book. He loved the story and agreed that the illustrations should be a clear representation of the writing. I'm blown away by what Vasya created, and I'm excited to work with him again on *Lily's Wondrous World: A Day at the Beach*, which should be out in the fall.

In addition to entertaining children, Lily's Wondrous World also emphasizes the importance of spending time with loved ones and exploring the outdoors. How do you see books like yours contributing to children's development and well-being?

Reading is crucial for intellectual development during a child's formative years, but it's also important in providing perspective. The message in my story is to explore nature and to connect with others. My book focuses on connections with animals, but children should apply the same principle to making friends with kids their age.

Can you share any insights or advice for aspiring writers who are looking to embark on their own creative journeys, especially those who may be transitioning from different professional backgrounds like yourself?

Tell the story that speaks to you. I wrote this book because my wife's story inspired me and I wanted to share it with everyone. I would tell other aspiring writers to read as much as they can and write about the things that interest them.

animals and seems to intuitively understand them, which is why they are drawn to her. It has always been this way according to my wife and her siblings. As a child, Elizabeth could often be found in the park feeding rabbits and squirrels. From a young age my wife has also had a love of horses and has ridden dressage for many years, even training at a prestigious school in France. When I wrote this book, I was imagining what a day of play was like for her while growing up. As for me, I also enjoyed being out in nature. I would walk the trails of Gladwyne, taking photos of deer, rabbits and the occasional fox.

From Jakarta to Bestseller

JESSE SUTANTO

A Journey Through Humour, Mystery, and Family Dynamics

Jesse Sutanto is a Chinese-Indonesian author. As of 2023, she has published nine novels for adults, young adults, and middle grade readers. She is most famous for her novel Dial A for Aunties, which won the 2021 Comedy Women in Print Prize and has been optioned for a film by Netflix.

BY BEN F. ONCU

Author Jesse Sutanto discusses her writing journey, inspirations behind Dial A for Aunties, familial themes, cinematic approach, Netflix adaptation, and upcoming releases, offering a glimpse into her captivating world.

Jesse Sutanto, a luminary in both children's and adult literature, weaves narratives that resonate with humour, mystery, and familial depth. Raised in Indonesia and Singapore, she brings a rich cultural tapestry to her storytelling, now based in Jakarta with her family. In an exclusive interview with Reader's House magazine, Jesse shares her journey from a crisis-ridden undergrad to a Master's graduate from the University of Oxford, where she found solace and purpose in the realm of creative writing.

Dial A for Aunties, Jesse's debut novel, stands as a testament to her ingenuity, blending humour and mystery with familial drama. Delving into the inspiration behind this acclaimed work, Jesse reveals a personal connection—a desire to explore her own family dynamics but with a twist that lends the necessary distance for creative exploration. It's this infusion of personal experience that infuses her work with authenticity and relatability.

Her background in film and television production adds another layer to her storytelling. While Jesse humbly dismisses her lack of hands-on production experience, she admits to crafting her novels with a cinematic lens. Her stories unfold like scenes in a movie, a testament to her visual storytelling prowess.

Excitingly, Dial A for Aunties has been optioned for adaptation into a Netflix movie, marking a significant milestone in Jesse's career. As the screenwriter crafts the adaptation, Jesse's input ensures cultural nuances are authentically captured—a testament to her dedication to representation and authenticity.

Looking ahead, Jesse tantalizes readers with upcoming releases, including the much-anticipated final instalment of the Aunties series, The Good, The Bad, and

Continued *on page 12*

STAR INTERVIEW

" Jesse Sutanto, acclaimed author of "Dial A for Aunties," shares insights into her writing process and upcoming projects in an exclusive interview with Reader's House magazine.

Continued *from page 10*

STAR INTERVIEW

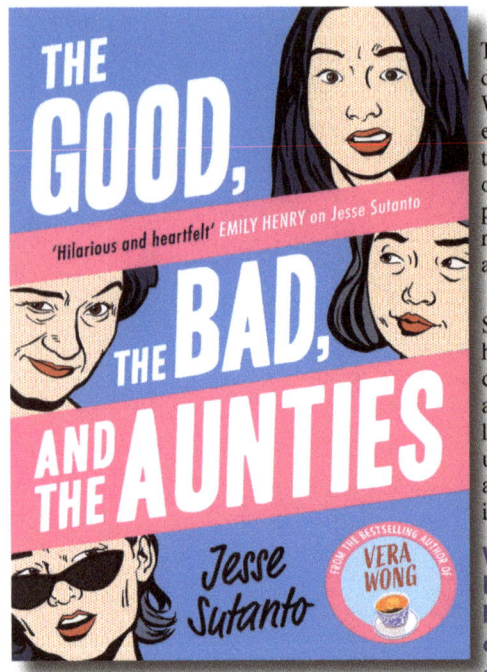

Jesse Q. Sutanto's *The Good, the Bad, and the Aunties* is a delightful conclusion to the Aunties series, blending humor, mystery, and family dynamics into a thoroughly entertaining read. Set against the vibrant backdrop of Jakarta during Chinese New Year, the story follows Meddy Chan, her new husband Nathan, and her hilariously meddlesome aunties as they navigate a series of chaotic and comical events.

Sutanto's writing shines with wit and charm, making the reader laugh out loud at the aunties' antics while also keeping them on the edge of their seat with the unfolding mystery. The characters are endearing and relatable, and their interactions are filled with warmth and humor. The plot is fast-paced and engaging, with plenty of twists and turns to keep readers hooked.

Overall, *The Good, the Bad, and the Aunties* is a heartwarming and laugh-out-loud funny book that beautifully wraps up the series. It's a must-read for fans of cozy mysteries and anyone looking for a feel-good story with a lot of heart.

The Aunties, alongside a dark suspense thriller, You Will Never Be Me. With each new work, Jesse continues to push boundaries, offering readers fresh perspectives and thrilling narratives that captivate and entertain.

In her work, Jesse Sutanto seamlessly blends humour, mystery, and cultural insight, leaving an indelible mark on literature. As her journey unfolds, readers eagerly anticipate the next chapter in her literary odyssey.

What inspired you to become a writer, and how did you embark on your journey as an author?

The honest answer is I had a bit of a crisis on the last year of my undergrad studies when I realized I was very much not ready for "the real world." I decided to apply to graduate programs and was accepted to the Masters in Creative Writing program at Oxford, which is honestly still very surreal to me!

Your debut novel, *Dial A for Aunties*, has garnered widespread acclaim. Can you share the inspiration behind the story and its unique blend of humour and mystery?

I've always wanted to write about my family, but whenever I tried writing about them, the drama had always hit too close to home, so I shelved the idea for a long while. Then one day, I thought: What if I threw a dead body into the story? And somehow, that gave me enough distance from the characters to really dive into it. It was the most natural I've felt writing a book. Whenever I got stuck in a scene, I'd think: What would my parents do? What would my aunts and uncles do? And it all would just start flowing.

Family dynamics play a significant role in your work, what draws you to explore these themes, and how do you approach portraying familial relationships in your writing?

I think I'm always drawn to family dynamics because in my culture, we are extremely close to our families, to the point where, when I lived abroad, I found that people often had a hard time understanding how close-knit we are. There is so much meddling and so much influence within our families and I've always struggled to explain it to others. So with the Aunties books, I knew that family was going to be the biggest theme and I really wanted to just share my family with the world, and that is what I've done.

Your background in film and television production is intriguing. How has this experience influenced your approach to storytelling in your novels?

Well I haven't had any actual experience producing yet, haha! I've been lucky enough to sell the options to my books, but we haven't gone into production yet, but I will say that I always think about my books as movies as I write them. I envision myself sitting in the cinema, enjoying a show, and I ask myself: "What do I want to see on the screen right now?" and that's how I plan my scenes.

Dial A for Aunties has been optioned for adaptation into a television series. Can you tell us more about this exciting development and your involvement in the project?

It's actually been optioned by Netflix into a movie. They've hired a screenwriter who is working on the screen adaptation right now and it's been such an amazing process because she often emails me with questions like: "What do moms usually call their kids in Indonesian or Mandarin, what's a word that's similar to 'Honey' or 'Dear'?" And I just can't wait to see the screenplay!

You have some exciting upcoming novels this year? Can you tell us about them? What can readers expect from these books, and how do they differ from your previous work?

The third and final instalment in the Aunties series is coming out this month. It's called The Good, The

Jesse Sutanto, a masterful storyteller, blends humour, mystery, and cultural depth, captivating readers with her authentic, cinematic narratives.

Bad, and The Aunties, and it's such a bittersweet moment for me. Dial A for Aunties changed my life, no exaggeration, and I'm so grateful to be able to turn it into a trilogy. Later in the year, I have a dark suspense thriller coming out, called You Will Never Be Me, and it's a book about toxic mom influencers which my editor described as "completely bonkers," so I can't wait to have that come out into the world.

STAR INTERVIEW

JESSE SUTANTO

Jesse Sutanto is a Chinese-Indonesian author celebrated for her diverse and engaging novels. She grew up between Jakarta and Singapore and holds a Master's degree from Oxford. Her multicultural background deeply influences her writing, which spans adult, young adult, and middle-grade genres.

Her notable works include the bestselling 'Dial A for Aunties' series, 'The Obsession,' and 'Vera Wong's Unsolicited Advice for Murderers.' Jesse's stories often blend humor, mystery, and cultural insights, drawing inspiration from her large, vibrant family.

Despite a busy family life with two children, Jesse has successfully published nine novels as of 2023. She is active on social media, where she connects with her readers and shares updates about her work. Jesse's unique voice and cultural representation have earned her critical acclaim, including the prestigious Comedy Women in Print Prize. Her work continues to captivate a dedicated and growing fan base.

EDITOR'S NOTE

In the vast and ever-evolving landscape of literature, there are authors who shine bright, captivating readers with their unique storytelling prowess. This issue, we are thrilled to feature Jesse Sutanto on the cover of Reader's House magazine, and there are countless reasons why she rightfully claims her place among literary luminaries.

Jesse Sutanto is not just an author; she is a storyteller extraordinaire whose narratives transcend boundaries, blending humour, mystery, and cultural insight seamlessly. Her journey from a crisis-ridden undergrad to a Master's graduate from the University of Oxford showcases resilience and determination, qualities that resonate throughout her work.

At the heart of Jesse's storytelling lies an exploration of familial dynamics—a theme deeply rooted in her Indonesian heritage. Through her debut novel, *Dial A for Aunties*, Jesse invites readers into a world where chaos and murder collide with family bonds, offering a refreshing take on the mystery genre.

What sets Jesse apart is her cinematic approach to storytelling, honed by her background in film and television production. Her novels unfold like scenes from a movie, captivating readers with vivid imagery and captivating plot twists. It's this visual storytelling prowess that has garnered widespread acclaim for her work.

Moreover, Jesse's contributions extend beyond the written page. With *Dial A for Aunties* optioned for adaptation into a Netflix movie, she brings cultural nuances to the forefront, ensuring authentic representation—an essential aspect of diversity and inclusion in literature.

As we delve deeper into Jesse's world in this issue, we are reminded of the transformative power of storytelling. Through her characters and narratives, Jesse invites readers on a journey of self-discovery, laughter, and intrigue—a journey that leaves an indelible mark on the literary landscape.

In featuring Jesse Sutanto on our cover, we celebrate not just an author but a visionary whose stories inspire, entertain, and unite readers from all walks of life. Join us as we embark on this literary adventure with Jesse Sutanto, a beacon of creativity and imagination in the world of literature.

EDITOR'S CHOICE

NOVEL • STORY • LITERATURE

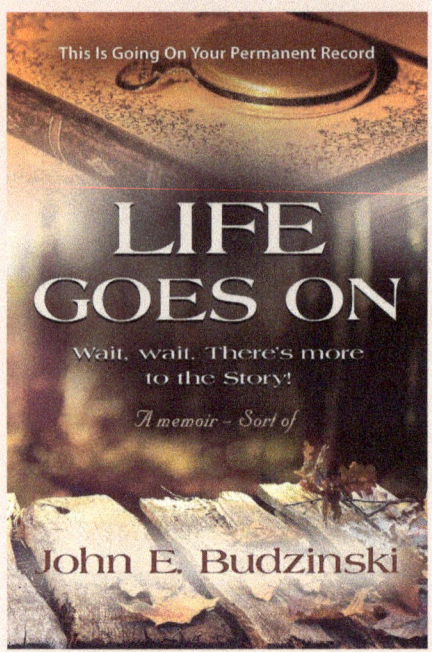

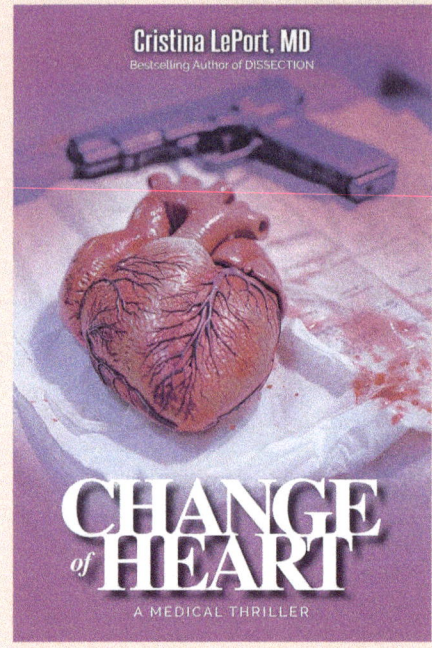

LIFE GOES ON
by John E. Budzinski

CHANGE OF HEART
by Cristina LePort

INDEPENDENCE
by Christopher C Tubbs

John E. Budzinski's 'Life Goes On' is a charming, witty exploration of life's simple moments with humor and poignant insights.

John E. Budzinski's *Life Goes On: Wait, wait. There's More to the Story!* is an engaging and thought-provoking exploration of one's personal legacy and the whims of fate. Through a series of whimsical and seemingly mundane anecdotes, Budzinski invites readers to ponder the mysteries of their own *Permanent Record* – that ominous ledger of life's actions and transgressions.

The book is structured around Budzinski's imaginative encounter with Saint Peter, who guides him through an audit of his life's moments before he faces *The Boss*. This clever narrative device allows Budzinski to reflect on various experiences such as spelling bees, blind dates, and dinner with strangers. These stories, though ordinary, are infused with humor and poignant insights, revealing deeper truths about the impact of our actions on ourselves and others.

Budzinski's conversational tone is both charming and disarming. His blend of sarcasm and sincere reflection creates a relatable and entertaining read. He skillfully balances over-telling and leaving gaps, prompting readers to engage actively with the narrative and fill in their own interpretations. This approach makes the reader a co-conspirator in his life's journey, enhancing the overall enjoyment and connection to the text.

The humor is well-timed, and even the predictable punchlines evoke genuine laughter. Budzinski's reflections are not just personal musings but resonate with universal themes of accountability, legacy, and the quest for personal redemption. He artfully reminds us that our simplest actions often hold more significance than we realize, and his candid self-assessment encourages readers to consider their own legacies with both seriousness and humor.

In essence, LIFE GOES ON is a delightful read that combines wit, wisdom, and a touch of cynicism. It's a gentle reminder that while we may all be "victims of circumstance," there's always more to our stories – and sometimes, the best we can do is laugh at the absurdity of it all.

Change of Heart is a masterful blend of medical expertise and thrilling suspense, keeping readers captivated from start to finish.

Change of Heart by Dr. Cristina LePort is a riveting addition to the medical thriller genre, seamlessly blending the high-stakes world of organ trafficking with the relentless pursuit of justice. Set against the vibrant backdrop of New York City, the novel kicks off with the tragic death of Amy Winter, a promising pre-med student whose heart continues to beat, symbolizing both hope and danger.

Detective Kirk Miner is thrust into a complex investigation that quickly spirals into a chilling conspiracy involving organ donations. The plot thickens with the introduction of FBI Agent Jack Mulville and Special Agent Charlotte Bloom, who join forces with Miner to unravel a web of corruption and deceit. The trio's dynamic is compelling, as they navigate the shadowy underbelly of organ trafficking, facing moral dilemmas and personal risks at every turn.

Dr. LePort's medical expertise shines through, adding a layer of authenticity and depth to the narrative. Her detailed knowledge of modern medicine and the ethical quandaries surrounding organ transplants enrich the story, making it both informative and thrilling. The novel's pacing is impeccable, with each chapter leaving you eager to uncover the next piece of the puzzle.

Change of Heart is more than just a thriller; it's a thought-provoking exploration of the lengths to which people will go to secure life-saving transplants. The characters are well-developed, each grappling with their own personal demons while striving to protect innocent lives. The moral complexities they face add a profound dimension to the story, elevating it beyond a simple crime novel.

Dr. Cristina LePort has crafted a masterful tale that will keep readers on the edge of their seats. Her ability to intertwine medical intricacies with suspenseful storytelling makes *Change of Heart* a standout in the genre. Whether you're a fan of medical dramas or crime thrillers, this book is a must-read. Prepare to be captivated from the first page to the last, as you join Miner, Mulville, and Bloom on their quest for justice in a world where every heartbeat counts.

Independence by Christopher C. Tubbs is a thrilling blend of naval warfare, espionage, and historical intrigue. A must-read masterpiece!

Independence: The Dorset Boy Book 16 by Christopher C. Tubbs is a masterful blend of historical fiction, naval warfare, and espionage set against the backdrop of the Greek War of Independence in 1827. Tubbs vividly portrays the geopolitical complexities of the era, where the Ottomans, Egyptians, and great powers like Britain, Russia, and France are entangled in a struggle for control and influence.

The story follows Vice Admiral Martin Stockley, who is tasked with commanding the Mediterranean Fleet to enforce the Treaty of London, leading to the pivotal Battle of Navarino. Tubbs' depiction of naval battles is both thrilling and meticulously detailed, capturing the tension and strategy of maritime warfare.

Parallel to Martin's naval exploits, the narrative delves into the world of espionage with Martin's unexpected promotion to head of the Foreign and Overseas Branch of British Intelligence after the tragic death of James Turner. Tubbs explores Martin's adaptation to his new role and the innovative espionage techniques he brings to the service.

Adding depth to the story is Martin's son, James, who continues the family's maritime legacy as part of the Ionian Patrol. His fascination with the emerging steam technology introduces readers to the dawn of a new era in naval history.

Independence is a captivating read, rich in historical detail and character development, making it a must-read for fans of historical and naval fiction.

NOVEL • STORY • LITERATURE   EDITOR'S CHOICE

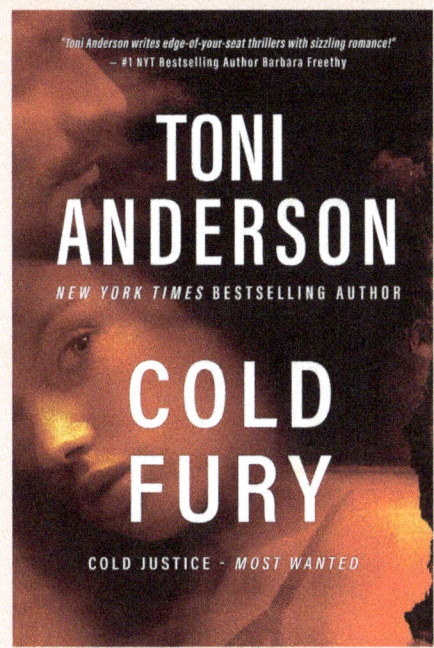

COLD FURY
by Toni Anderson

COURAGE OF ONE
by Zola Blue

BEAUTIFUL AND TERRIBLE THINGS
by S.M. Stevens

Cold Fury is a thrilling masterpiece, blending intense suspense and heartfelt romance, keeping readers captivated from start to finish.

Courage of One is a masterful blend of fantasy, adventure, and romance, with rich characters and an enthralling plot.

Beautiful and Terrible Things is a masterful blend of friendship, self-discovery, and social justice, offering profound insights and heartfelt storytelling.

Cold Fury: A Romantic Thriller by Toni Anderson is a gripping addition to the Cold Justice® - Most Wanted series that masterfully blends suspense, romance, and relentless action. The story centers on Hope Harper, a former star defense attorney whose life was shattered when a wrongfully released defendant murdered her family. Now an Assistant District Attorney, Hope is driven by a singular mission: to ensure that no other family suffers as hers did.

The plot thickens when the same serial killer escapes from a maximum-security prison during a brutal winter storm, setting his sights on revenge. Enter Aaron Nash, an FBI Hostage Rescue Team operator assigned to protect Hope. Despite her refusal to go into protective custody, Aaron is determined to keep her safe. Their initial friction gradually gives way to mutual respect and a burgeoning attraction, adding a layer of emotional depth to the high-stakes narrative.

Anderson's skillful storytelling keeps readers on the edge of their seats, weaving together intense action scenes with moments of poignant vulnerability. The chemistry between Hope and Aaron is palpable, and their evolving relationship adds a compelling dimension to the thriller. As the killer's rampage continues, the tension escalates, leading to a heart-pounding climax that will leave readers breathless.

Cold Fury is a must-read for fans of romantic thrillers, offering a perfect blend of danger, passion, and resilience. Toni Anderson delivers a powerful story of survival and second chances that will stay with you long after the final page.

Courage of One by Zola Blue is a captivating tale that seamlessly blends elements of fantasy, adventure, and romance. Set in ancient times, the story introduces readers to the Dragonors, a noble race that competes in deadly tournaments to gain status. The protagonist, Luken, a humble blacksmith, enters the competition with the hope of winning the hand of Talulah, the village lord's daughter. Despite his lack of experience, Luken's determination and the aid of Talulah's dragon lead him to an unexpected victory.

The narrative takes a poignant turn as the happiness of Luken and Talulah is shattered by the invasion of men, leading to Talulah's tragic death. The Dragonors, choosing peace over vengeance, leave Earth and form alliances with the Mejuarian and the Arvunglies in their new home. These alliances are tested when King Teloby's mewling nests go missing, prompting a daring rescue mission.

Zola Blue masterfully weaves a rich tapestry of interconnected stories, from the Dragonors' ancient traditions to the modern-day discovery of the nests by a young boy named Ren. The characters are well-developed, and the plot is filled with unexpected twists and heartfelt moments. *Courage of One* is a testament to bravery, love, and the power of unlikely friendships. It is a must-read for fans of epic fantasy and adventure.

S.M. Stevens' *Beautiful and Terrible Things* is a poignant exploration of friendship, self-discovery, and the harsh realities of contemporary American life. The novel centers on Charley Byrne, a 29-year-old who has retreated into a life of isolation, managing a bookstore and hiding from a seven-year curse. Her world begins to expand when she meets Xander Wallace, a quirky activist who introduces her to a diverse group of friends.

Stevens masterfully crafts a narrative that is both enlightening and entertaining. Charley's journey from social exile to active participation in social justice movements is compelling and relatable. The diverse cast of characters, each with their unique backgrounds and struggles, adds depth and authenticity to the story. The novel does an excellent job of portraying the vibrancy and challenges of life in a major city, touching on issues of race, gender, and sexual orientation with sensitivity and insight.

However, the story takes a darker turn as Charley faces betrayals that threaten her sanctuary—the bookstore—and push her into a dangerous depression. Stevens handles these themes with care, highlighting the transformative power of friendship while also acknowledging its potential to cause pain.

Beautiful and Terrible Things is a beautifully crafted story that reminds us of the complexities of human connections and the resilience required to navigate life's challenges. It's a must-read for anyone interested in contemporary fiction that tackles real-world issues with grace and empathy.

EDITOR'S CHOICE

NOVEL • STORY • LITERATURE

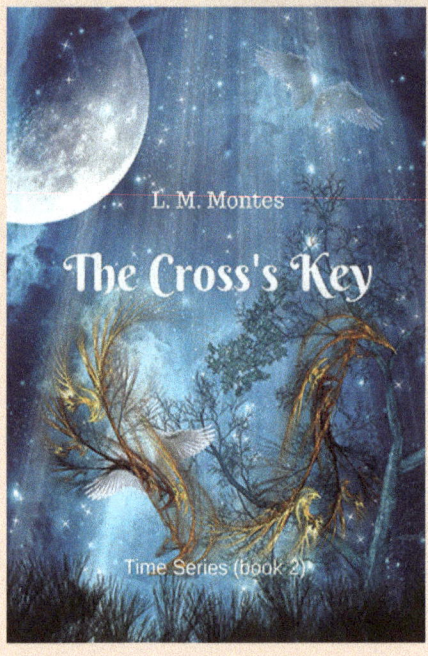

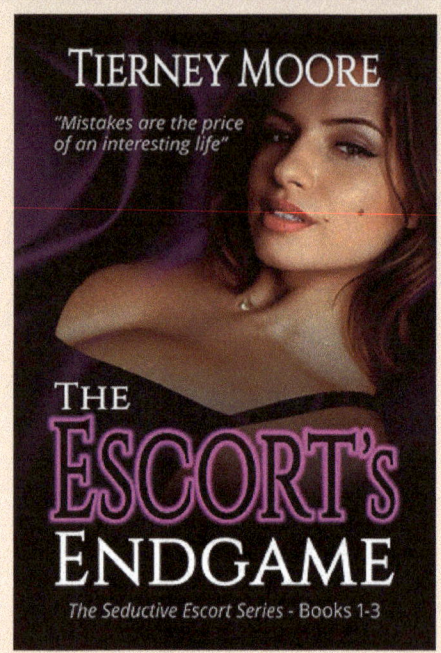

HARVARD
by Kirsten Pursell

THE CROSS'S KEY
by L. M. Montes

THE ESCORT'S ENDGAME
by Tierney Moore

Harvard by Kirsten Pursell is a beautifully written, emotionally resonant novel with compelling characters and a richly detailed setting. Highly recommended!

Kirsten Pursell's *Harvard* is a compelling and beautifully written novel that captures the essence of ambition, love, and the struggle to overcome one's past. The story revolves around Helena *Harvard* Schmitt, a young woman who escapes her life on the mountain through her extraordinary talent for running, which earns her a place at the prestigious Harvard University. There, she encounters Thor Himmel, a figure who seems almost too perfect to be real—attractive, intelligent, and seemingly unattainable.

Pursell's writing is both engaging and evocative, drawing readers into the complex lives of her characters. Helena's journey is particularly inspiring, as she navigates the pressures of academic life and the emotional turmoil of her past. Thor, on the other hand, is a fascinating character whose own struggles and vulnerabilities make him more than just a handsome face.

The novel excels in its exploration of themes such as resilience, the impact of past traumas, and the power of human connection. The chemistry between Helena and Thor is palpable, and their interactions are filled with tension and tenderness. Pursell does an excellent job of developing their relationship in a way that feels authentic and deeply moving.

One of the standout aspects of *Harvard* is its setting. The depiction of Harvard University is rich and detailed, providing a vivid backdrop for the story. The contrast between Helena's rugged mountain upbringing and the elite academic environment adds depth to her character and highlights her determination and adaptability.

While the novel is generally well-paced, there are moments where the narrative slows down, which might test the patience of some readers. However, these slower sections are often filled with introspective passages that add to the overall depth of the story.

Harvard is a thought-provoking and emotionally resonant novel that will appeal to readers who enjoy character-driven stories with a strong sense of place. Kirsten Pursell has crafted a memorable tale of love, redemption, and the courage to face one's demons. Highly recommended for fans of contemporary fiction and romance.

L. M. Montes's The Cross's Key is a thrilling, immersive adventure with rich characters and a gripping, supernatural plot. Highly recommended!

The Cross's Key by L. M. Montes is a masterful continuation of the Time Series that will leave readers on the edge of their seats. From the very first page, Montes weaves a tale of suspense, adventure, and supernatural intrigue that is impossible to put down.

The protagonist, Kyle Stevens, finds himself in a precarious situation after blacking out in the Cave of Treasures and awakening in a different realm. The vivid and historical events unfolding before him are both mesmerizing and horrifying, pulling readers into a world where the past and present collide in the most unexpected ways. Montes's ability to create such a rich and immersive setting is truly commendable.

One of the standout elements of this book is the reappearance of a long-forgotten relic from Kyle's past, which adds layers of mystery and urgency to the narrative. The quest that Kyle must undertake is fraught with danger and moral dilemmas, especially with the malevolent presence of Lord Ladonnis, an evil angel whose sinister plans could cost Kyle his very soul.

Montes excels in character development, particularly with Kyle, whose internal struggles and dedication to his teaching career make him a relatable and compelling hero. The tension between his desire for a normal life and the unavoidable quest he must face is palpable and adds depth to his character.

The pacing of the story is perfect, with each chapter building on the last, leading to a climax that is both satisfying and leaves readers eagerly anticipating the next installment. The blend of historical elements with supernatural themes is executed flawlessly, making *The Cross's Key* a standout in the genre.

In conclusion, *The Cross's Key* is a must-read for fans of supernatural thrillers and historical fiction. L. M. Montes has crafted a gripping and unforgettable tale that will captivate readers from start to finish. Highly recommended!

A thrilling blend of suspense and steamy romance, The Escort's Endgame captivates with rich characters and evocative settings.

The Escort's Endgame by Tierney Moore is a captivating blend of suspense, romance, and erotica that keeps readers on the edge of their seats. As the fourth installment in *"The Seductive Escort Series,"* this book delves deep into the life of Miranda Stewart, a high-end escort with a dark past and a glamorous present.

Miranda, or Miri, is a complex character who has risen from the depths of homelessness to the heights of luxury, navigating the elite circles of Europe with grace and allure. Her encounters, especially with her female clients, are depicted with a sensuality that is both steamy and emotionally charged. Moore's writing vividly brings to life the opulence of Miri's world, from luxury hotels to superyachts, making for an immersive reading experience.

The suspense element is skillfully woven into the narrative as Miri's past threatens to unravel her carefully constructed life. The introduction of a new, alluring woman adds an unexpected twist, challenging Miri's notions of love and security. The chemistry between them is palpable, adding depth to the erotic scenes that are both explicit and tastefully done.

The Escort's Endgame is more than just a tale of erotic escapades; it's a story of liberation and self-discovery. With its rich character development, thrilling plot, and evocative settings, this book is a must-read for fans of romantic erotica and suspense. Moore's ability to balance steamy romance with a gripping storyline makes this a standout addition to the series.

NOVEL • STORY • LITERATURE

EDITOR'S CHOICE

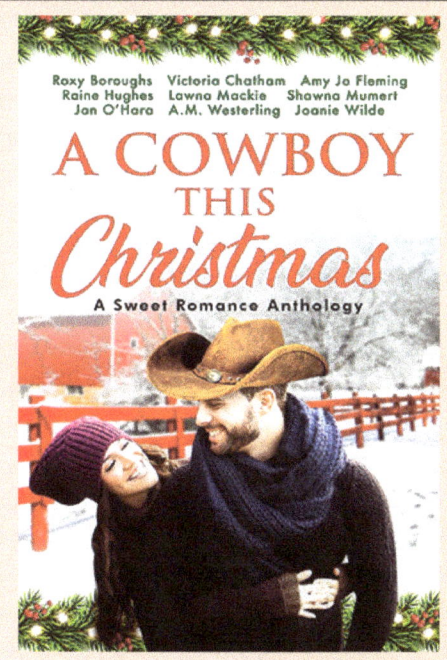

A COWBOY THIS CHRISTMAS
by Roxy Boroughs, Victoria Chatham

THEIR CONNECTICUT CONCUBINE
by Karen Nappa

A NEW DAWNING
by Janice Angelique

A Cowboy This Christmas is a heartwarming anthology, perfect for holiday romance lovers seeking sweet, uplifting, and festive stories.

A captivating blend of romance and erotica, Their Connecticut Concubine is an emotional, steamy, and unforgettable journey. Highly recommended!

A New Dawning is a masterful blend of love, family secrets, and redemption, captivating readers with its emotional depth and twists.

A Cowboy This Christmas is a delightful collection of nine heartwarming stories that capture the magic of the holiday season. Each tale, penned by talented authors like Jan O'Hara, Roxy Boroughs, and Victoria Chatham, offers a unique blend of romance, hope, and the spirit of Christmas.

The anthology opens with *The Cowboy's Comeback Christmas,* where Jan O'Hara introduces us to a couple with a past, navigating the complexities of second chances. Roxy Boroughs' *Capturing the Christmas Cowboy* follows, bringing a city photographer and a rugged rancher together in a charming, festive setting.

Raine Hughes' *A Rocking Horse Christmas* and A.M. Westerling's *Candy Cane Cowboy* continue the theme of healing and love, each story rich with emotional depth and holiday cheer. Victoria Chatham's *All I Want for Christmas* is a touching narrative about finding family and love in unexpected places.

Lawna Mackie's *Silver Belle*'s Christmas Cowboy adds a dash of adventure, while Shawna Mumert's *My Cowboy, Until Christmas* and Amy Jo Fleming's *Come Home for Christmas, Cowboy* explore themes of resilience and rekindled love. Joanie Wilde's *A Heart Creek Christmas* rounds out the collection with a tender story of overcoming personal barriers.

A Cowboy This Christmas is a perfect read for anyone looking to immerse themselves in sweet, uplifting romances set against the backdrop of the holiday season. Each story is a testament to the enduring power of love and the magic of Christmas.

Karen Nappa's *Their Connecticut Concubine* is a sizzling, emotional rollercoaster that takes readers on a journey through unexpected romance, intense passion, and heart-wrenching choices.

Elizabeth Brook, the protagonist, steps into a new job expecting to care for an elderly man, only to find herself in the company of a brooding, former hockey player and his equally dominant manager. The chemistry between Elizabeth and her new bosses is palpable from the start, and Nappa masterfully weaves a tale of erotic discovery and emotional depth.

The characters are well-developed, with Elizabeth's transformation from a caregiver to a woman exploring the depths of her desires being particularly compelling. The former hockey player and his manager are not just eye candy; they bring their own complexities and vulnerabilities to the story, making the romantic entanglements feel genuine and deeply engaging.

Nappa's writing is both steamy and sophisticated, balancing the erotic elements with a storyline that keeps you hooked. The world of pain and pleasure that Elizabeth is introduced to is described with a mix of allure and authenticity, making it easy for readers to get lost in the fantasy.

However, the book isn't just about passion. Elizabeth's responsibilities and the tough choices she faces add a layer of realism and emotional weight to the narrative. When the unthinkable happens, the stakes are raised, and readers are left on the edge of their seats, wondering how Elizabeth will navigate her conflicting loyalties.

Their Connecticut Concubine is a captivating read that blends romance, erotica, and drama seamlessly. Karen Nappa has crafted a story that is as heartwarming as it is heart-pounding, making it a must-read for fans of contemporary romance with a daring twist.

A New Dawning by Janice Angelique is a captivating and emotionally charged novel that masterfully intertwines themes of love, family secrets, and personal redemption. From the very first page, Angelique draws readers into the complex lives of her characters, making it nearly impossible to put the book down.

The story centers around Angela, the heiress to a prosperous supermarket chain in the San Fernando Valley. Her life takes an unexpected turn when she meets Martin Richardson, a charming doctor who mistakes her for a cashier. This seemingly innocent misunderstanding sets the stage for a deeply engaging narrative.

Angela's character is both relatable and inspiring. She navigates the challenges of her privileged yet complicated life with grace and determination. Her relationship with Martin is beautifully portrayed, highlighting the nuances of love and trust. Martin, on the other hand, is a man haunted by his past, and his journey towards healing and acceptance is both poignant and compelling.

One of the standout aspects of *A New Dawning* is the intricate family dynamics. Angela's relationship with her domineering mother adds a layer of tension and drama that keeps readers on the edge of their seats. The revelation of a long-kept family secret further intensifies the plot, leading to a dramatic clash between mother and daughter, and sister against sister.

Janice Angelique's writing is both elegant and evocative. She has a talent for creating vivid scenes and complex characters that stay with you long after you've finished the book. The emotional depth and the unexpected twists and turns make *A New Dawning* a truly memorable read.

A New Dawning is a beautifully written novel that explores the complexities of love, family, and personal growth. Janice Angelique has crafted a story that is both heartwarming and heartbreaking, leaving readers with a sense of hope and renewal. This book is a must-read for anyone who enjoys a well-told story with rich character development and a gripping plot. Highly recommended!

Exploring the Skies and Fields with

REBECCA VICTOR

A Voice of Courage, Gratitude, and Rural Inspiration

Rebecca Victor, author and mother, shares her inspirations from rural upbringing, family values, and her daughters, crafting educational yet entertaining children's books fostering literacy and imagination.

Nestled in the heart of Wiggins, Colorado, author Rebecca Victor paints the landscape of her childhood memories with strokes of courage, gratitude, and rural charm. Married to her best friend Ronnie, and a mother to three inspiring daughters—Mya, Ellie, and Tessa—Rebecca's journey into the world of children's literature is a testament to the power of family, resilience, and the magic of storytelling.

From the humble confines of her 900 square foot farmhouse to the boundless skies above, Rebecca's upbringing in a farming community laid the fertile soil for her literary aspirations. Surrounded by the warmth of family tales and the backdrop of the Buckingham Ranch, Rebecca imbibed the spirit of adventure and the value of hard work, shaping her into the storyteller she is today.

With a backdrop steeped in aviation, Rebecca's books soar to new heights, with characters like Ellie, Tessa, and Mya taking centre stage in tales of bravery, gratitude, and cultural exploration. Inspired by her daughters and their diverse interests, each character embodies a facet of Rebecca's own journey—be it resilience in the face of adversity, the courage to embrace one's uniqueness, or the gratitude for life's blessings, no matter how challenging the circumstances.

But Rebecca's stories transcend mere entertainment—they serve as windows into worlds both familiar and unknown, educating young readers about the wonders of agriculture, aviation, and diverse cultures. Through meticulous research and personal anecdotes, Rebecca weaves a tapestry of learning and discovery, inviting children to explore, question, and dream.

Yet, perhaps the most rewarding chapter of Rebecca's literary voyage lies in the classrooms and communities she touches. As she shares her books with eager minds and curious hearts, Rebecca fosters a love for literacy that transcends the pages of her stories, inspiring children to embrace their creativity and imagination in a world often dominated by screens.

Looking ahead, Rebecca's pen is poised to craft new adventures on the pages of children's literature, with upcoming projects delving into the world of dairy farming and beyond. With each story, she hopes to find a place on every bookshelf and in every classroom, enriching the lives of young readers and igniting the spark of imagination that lies within each child.

In a world where the rush of daily life often drowns out the whispers of storytelling, Rebecca Victor stands as a beacon of hope—a storyteller who reminds us of the magic found in the simplest of tales and the power of courage, gratitude, and rural inspiration.

What inspired you to write children's books, particularly focusing on themes of courage and gratitude?

I have always wanted to write a children's book and because I'm in the dental field I always thought it would be something in that genre.

> Take flight with 'Ellie The Crop Duster Saves The Farm,' where courage and gratitude soar high above the fields, inspiring young hearts to reach for the skies.

However, when I became a mother and our youngest was diagnosed with autism her preference was any book that had something to do with modes of transportation. After reading all that we could find in the local libraries and amazon, I noticed a big gap in the aviation related books and so, I chose planes. I specifically chose little girl planes because of my three girls, but I also feel like aviation has been a field that strong and determined women have always been a part of. As for the themes of courage and gratitude, we always try to teach that to our girls. There's always something to be thankful for, even in the tough times. My grandpa, before he passed away, would remind me every time we would end a visit or a phone call "Sis, don't forget to count your blessings" and so that's become my mantra, trying to see the good and the light in the experience no matter how hard it is. This hasn't always been easy. In 2019, a distracted driver hit us at a stop light traveling 65mph and the worst of Mya's injuries was a moderate brain injury, Tessa's autism diagnosis followed the car accident, and I suffered my own injuries physically, but emotionally as a momma, this was the hardest thing we've had to go through to date. Thankfully Ellie wasn't in the vehicle that day or the spare tire that ended up in her car seat would have been a deadly outcome.

How do you incorporate your own childhood experiences growing up in a farming community into your stories?

I didn't always appreciate growing up on the farm, in fact as a kid I often grumbled about having to help out during those long summer days when my classmates and friends were at the baseball field. However, the work ethic I gained, the freedom from things that now tie our younger generations to screens inhibiting their sense of adventure and discovery, and the time we shared as a family even in the hot and sweaty hay field, is something my husband and I are working towards getting our family back into the country and into the dirt! Agriculture is such an important and yet dying industry in today's society, so I'm hoping to inspire and share the love of it with readers young and old! In Ellie The Crop Duster Saves The Farm, my love and nod towards my little family farm shines through as our farm dog Roman stars in the story, Miss Frizzle is inspired by a chicken we had growing up, and my mom is illustrated in the pumpkin patch (the woman holding the pumpkin in the air). I'm currently working on my next book that will also highlight a different area of the agriculture industry but this time on a dairy farm. In the fall I would work in the scale house at our local dairy weighing silage trucks and we live in an area of Colorado where there are 5 or 6 dairies and feedlots within a 10-15 mile radius.

Can you tell us about the process of creating your characters, such as Ellie, Tessa, and Mya?

I was going to start with just one book, but with 3 girls, how do you just pick one?! So Ellie became a crop duster, Tessa became an airtanker, and Mya a plane on an island. I chose Ellie for the book cantered around farming because she is my brave and determined one, the one I see myself in the most as far as her "farm girl" traits. Not afraid to pick up the toads or get dirty helping with the garden or whatever the task is, she will do it with courage and grit. Tessa's character, the air tanker, came from her love of all things firefighting. My dad, his brothers and their dad were all Denver Firefighters, so maybe that's where her love for fire fighters come from. Tessa's character is also a reflection of her determination and struggle as a kiddo on the autism spectrum, she is often misunderstood by her peers, and yet her intelligence and way she perceives the world has stopped me in my tracks with appreciation and awe so often. Mya, as I mentioned, suffered a moderate brain injury at the age of 7. She has had and continues to overcome difficulties that aren't often seen (like a cast on a broken arm) and so I wanted her character to demonstrate gratitude and seeing things from a different perspective when she ends up in a situation that she wouldn't have chosen for herself. My husband Ronnie also grew up in the Caribbean on the island of Trinidad, so I wanted to highlight a different culture and dialect in one of my stories. I chose Curacao specialty after finding a blog about an airplane that someone had carried the pieces of into the jungle and had planned to turn into a kitchen, however, plans must have changed and now it's overgrown with plants and jungle.

What message do you hope young readers take away from your books?

I hope young readers take away the love of reading and learning about different things or cultures, and that it inspires them to even write down their own creations. That's why I chose my motto to be, "Inspiring the love of literacy one character, one story, and one book at a time."

How do you approach writing stories that are both entertaining and educational for children?

I love to read and I think the stories that I love the most are the ones that make me think a little deeper or learn something or see something in a new and interesting way that I haven't experienced before. So with all of my books I wanted to do the same. For Ellie's book, I reached out to our local pumpkin farm for information about how crop dusting is used in pumpkin farming as well more about crop dusting including the history and different ways crop dusting planes can be used. In Tessa's research, living in Colorado we often have wildfires, so I wanted to learn more about aerial firefighters and how they are used in fighting fires. For Mya's book, I wanted to be sure that the animals I picked were unique but also that they lived on the island. In Colorado we have lots of deer, but I wondered how on earth did a deer get to an island? I also felt like it was important to not only highlight another culture, their people of history (like Tula), and their dialect that makes them unique.

What has been the most rewarding aspect of sharing your books with classrooms and readers?

Sharing my books with schools whether it's in the classroom or a bigger group presentation have been my favourite part of being an author so far! I love seeing their eager listening ears and inquisitive questions that not only get them thinking, but me too! I hope that I can inspire them to write their own stories and step outside of the world of screens where creativity and imagination are being robbed from their childhoods.

Are there any upcoming projects or new characters you're excited to introduce to your readers?

I am currently working on researching for my 4th book centred around a dairy farm. There are things like murmuration (the term used to describe the groups of birds that fly above dairy farms) and help readers understand where their food comes from when they open their refrigerator. Something that I again would love to help little readers learn about and older readers enjoy with silly puns and "old time" phrases that I often hear from my grandma Shirely as a nod to the old days! I am considering having the main character in this story be a tractor and Ellie just be a guest in her part of dairy farming.

How do you see your books fitting into the larger landscape of children's literature, and what sets them apart?

I think every author's dream would be to have their books on every bookshelf or bedside table, and be in every classroom or school library, so that's my dream too. I also try to make my stories unique with the additional information in the back of the stories, adding personal connections that I can share in more detail to my school groups, and adding the fun worksheets that go with each story on my website for families or schools to print and do together as a family. I don't know if there's anything that warms my heart more than to hear my girls read to me or to pull my little nieces and nephew into my lap and read them a story. You can't beat that time together and the bonding that happens around a story book.

Embracing Life's Adventures
GLENDA MITCHELL
From Health Crisis to Intentional Living, Unveiling the Journey of Kicking Out The Bucket

Glenda Mitchell shares her transformative journey from a health crisis to intentional living, inspiring readers to seize life's opportunities

In a world often characterized by routine and predictability, Glenda Mitchell stands out as a beacon of adventure and inspiration. Describing herself as an adventure-seeking, marathon-running traveler, Glenda infuses every aspect of her life with a relentless pursuit of challenge and growth. But behind her remarkable feats lies a story of resilience and transformation.

In 2016, Glenda faced a significant health scare that forced her to confront her priorities and embrace a more balanced approach to living. This pivotal moment became the catalyst for her introspection, prompting her to celebrate her accomplishments while realigning her focus with her core values. Out of this introspection emerged her book, *KICKING Out THE BUCKET List*, a deeply personal account that encourages readers to seize life's opportunities and chart their own path to fulfillment.

In our interview with Glenda, she shares candid insights into how her health crisis reshaped her perspective on life and motivated her to amplify her impact beyond her immediate circle. Her passion for community, travel, and adventure shines through as she discusses the delicate balance between pursuing personal passions and fostering connections with people from all walks of life.

Through her book, Glenda challenges readers to reflect on their own lives, celebrate their achievements, and embrace intentional living. She offers practical advice for those feeling stuck or uncertain, urging them to draw wisdom from their past while remaining focused on creating a fulfilling future.

Glenda's influence extends far beyond the pages of her book, as she continues to inspire individuals and groups to embrace change and pursue their true passions. Her hope is simple yet profound: to ignite a spark within others that will fuel a journey of self-discovery and positive impact.

As you embark on your own journey of self-discovery, may Glenda's words serve as a guiding light, empowering you to embrace life's challenges, celebrate your successes, and live with intentionality.

Your book "KICKING Out THE BUCKET List" is deeply personal, drawing from your own experiences, including a life-threatening health crisis. Can you share more about

GLENDA MITCHELL

KICKING Out THE BUCKET List by Glenda Mitchell inspires readers to live life to the fullest, embracing adventure and intentional living.

> Glenda Mitchell's story of resilience and adventure reminds us to embrace life fully and pursue our passions with intentionality.

how that event influenced your perspective on life and inspired you to write this book?

Before my health crisis, I was already very motivated and prepared to try almost anything. I had racked up a list of things that I had done that many people would only dream of. I became frustrated when people told me about the things they wanted to do and never did. I encouraged and supported them to "just do it". Following my health emergency, this desire to move others into action became stronger. I felt that writing a book would increase my reach outside my immediate circle, beyond friends, colleagues or clients.

Your passion for community, travel, and adventure shines through in your writing. How do you balance these pursuits with your desire for unity and connection with people from all walks of life?

I have found that being prepared to try a broad range of pursuits has allowed me to connect with a wide spectrum of people. Being able to hold my own in a running event has enabled me to build relationships with athletes. Being prepared to learn more about history and art has connected me with artists and enabled me to converse with friends in Europe. Prioritising time for people became a greater focus following my health crisis. I have had amazing conversations with people at airports and churches, on street corners and in art galleries. There are so many incredible places to visit and things to see, but no matter where I have been in the world, the defining factor has been the people.

In your book, you encourage readers to reflect on their own lives and celebrate their accomplishments. What advice do you have for individuals who may feel stuck or uncertain about how to pursue their passions and live more intentionally?

Most of us have heard or read advice to live in the moment and not let our past define our future. This is certainly true when we have failures and hurts that are holding us back. However, reflecting on our past can give insights into why we made the choices we did and even whether we would make the same choices again. This process of reflection has proven to be an invaluable method of helping someone establish what they are truly passionate about, providing a basis to make intentional choices about the future. It's not about allowing the past to define us but rather using it to inform us. Or to quote Winston Churchill, "Those who fail to learn from history are condemned to repeat it".

You've worked with individuals and groups, inspiring them to discover or rekindle their passions. Can you share a memorable experience where you've seen someone make a significant transformation in their life after embracing your guidance?

I have had the privilege of seeing many people embrace a change in their lives as a result of my influence. It would be unfair of me to take all the credit for any significant transformation. A major shift requires a concerted effort by the individual concerned. One instance does stand out for me. I helped one of my clients get back into running after he had tried unsuccessfully over many years. Not only did he finish the event that he set his sights on, but the impact turned out to be far greater. Soon after the race, he was diagnosed with advanced cancer and the doctors stated that his increased fitness levels were instrumental in bringing about what turned out to be a full recovery.

Your book challenges readers to disrupt their own lives and focus on what brings them true value and joy. How do you navigate the tension between societal expectations and personal fulfillment, and what strategies do you suggest for others facing similar struggles?

The world we live in thrives on a constant barrage of "experiences." Comparing your life to someone else's carefully curated Instagram feed is an exercise in futility. What matters is finding your unique version of richness, one that fuels your passions. By establishing and embracing your definition of "enough", learning to say "NO" to things that don't align with your values or that drain your resources, you can overcome the FOMO (Fear of Missing Out) trap.

As you continue to inspire others through your writing and community engagement, what are your hopes for the impact of KICKING Out THE BUCKET List, and what message do you hope readers will take away from it?

For readers to learn to be intentional about what they choose to do and intentional about actually

Reader's House || 23

PHOTO: *Joseph Seechack, acclaimed author and former television network operations expert, now delves into the world of literary fiction.*

Transitioning from Network Operations to Novel Writing

JOSEPH SEECHACK

Crafting Stories of Love, Loss, and Resilience

Joseph Seechack discusses his transition from television to writing, the emotional depth of his debut novel, and his unique approach to character development and storytelling.

In the world of literary fiction, few debut novels come with the kind of profound depth and emotional resonance as *A Love To Die For* by Joseph Seechack. Seechack, a seasoned veteran of television network operations, has turned his narrative talents inward, crafting stories that delve into the human condition with a rare blend of humor and heartache. After decades of honing his storytelling skills behind the scenes at ABC-TV Network and serving the City of New York, Seechack has embraced his long-held passion for writing, exploring the intricate layers of human experience through his prose.

Seechack's writing journey is rooted in a lifetime of personal exploration and a desire to understand the complexities of human nature. His stories, often sprinkled with moments of humor amidst the struggles of his characters, reflect his belief in the power of laughter and its ability to make life's trials more bearable. *A Love To Die For* stands as a testament to his literary philosophy, portraying a narrative that is as heartbreaking as it is uplifting. The novel follows the journey of Grace Butler, a woman shattered by the sudden loss of her husband, as she navigates the tumultuous path of grief and finds solace in the unwavering support of her friends.

In our interview, Seechack shares insights into his transition from a successful career in television to the world of novel writing, his approach to character development, and the inspiration behind his compelling debut. His reflections offer a glimpse into the mind of a writer who not only seeks to entertain but also to challenge and transform his readers. Join us as we delve into the creative process and personal philosophies of Joseph Seechack, a storyteller dedicated to exploring the depths of the human spirit.

What inspired you to transition from your career in television to becoming a novelist?

I worked in Television for 35 years. I was laid off from my last employer, ABC-TV Network. I then worked for the City of New York for eleven years before retiring. Being retired, I had fewer distractions, the time, the motivation and the need to write more seriously, more productively.

Your short story To Catch A Thief was included in the *Writers of Tomorrow* anthology. How did that experience influence your writing journey?

I am forever grateful to Ms. Ruchi Acharaya of Wingless Dreamer. She saw some talent

A Love To Die For by Joseph Seechack, a poignant debut novel exploring love, loss, and resilience.

and potential in me and included my story, in her short story anthology, *Writer of Tomorrow* which was published in 2021. That was tremendously encouraging and it gave me some validation and credibility in the marketplace. Thank you Ruchi.

A Love To Die For is your debut novel. Can you tell us a bit about the story and what readers can expect from it?

My debut novel, A Love To Die For will grab the readers by the collar with two hands and pull them into the story. I want readers to connect and FEEL, really FEEL and hopefully be changed and find hope and energy from the story.

A wonderful wife, Grace Butler, has found legendary true love with Ron, The One, the one true love of her life. If Love had a Mount Rushmore, they would be on it. She comes home to an empty house, and later learns that her husband has died, without a chance to say goodbye. Their kiss before she went out, was their last kiss.

She is far beyond devastated; she was annihilated. Her Perfect Love is dead. How will she survive with two fatherless children? How can she deliver a eulogy worthy of their incredible marriage? When she buried her husband, her heart pleaded to be buried with him, and so it was. She couldn't stand the idea of their hearts apart from one another.

How can she move on and try to build a new life for herself and her children?

Thank God she has been blessed with strong, amazing, loving girlfriends, who carry her along to some form of new life. Grace is the triumph of the individual over adversity. The triumph of love over death. In Time, she evolves to a place where she can teach others to move on with their lives like she has.

As readers, they cannot enter the story and help Grace. They can only struggle along with her and cheer her on and cry with her in her tortured struggle over the *Sudden Vacuum* in her life and in their legendary marriage. The reader will experience a Cathartic Release in seeing Grace overcome the endless, torture that her life become only to triumph, just by surviving and evolving into a new life thanks to her loving girlfriends. We are not powerless. We are not alone.

The only villain in my book, is Death itself, with the death of Ron. But death is the end of life, not the end of love. Love transcends death and moves on to a higher, more celestial level of loving, as readers will see.

You mentioned that you like to explore the strengths and weaknesses of your characters. How do you approach character development in your writing process?

Despite what you see on TV and in the movies, space is not the Final Frontier. People have been, and always will be the Final Frontier. Why do people do the things they do? *Tis a Puzzlement!*

I've been blessed with the ability to see through more than just my own eyes. I can see through the eyes of my characters, so that I can better tell their stories. I like my characters to face Moral Dilemmas, and see what choices they make. Moral Dilemmas explore the inner workings of the characters, and maybe the readers as well.

As a writer, I believe that a blank page is a new canvas for a writer, an invitation to adventure, for the writer as well as the reader. The blank page is an entirely limitless universe before me. My mind is my own Starship Enterprise.

I like to write myself into a corner, if it helps the story. Then I have to figure out how to write myself out of that corner to advance the plot and move the story along. I believe that the more ways you look at a problem, the

> Seechack masterfully blends humour and heartache, crafting compelling narratives that resonate deeply with readers, showcasing his exceptional storytelling talent.

greater the number of solutions become visible.

Your writing style is described as artistic and focused on arranging words and ideas into beautifully orchestrated sentences. Can you share a bit about your approach to crafting prose?

I write what I feel. I write what I know, what I've lived. I really love humour. I believe that God has a sense of humour. That is where my sense of humour comes from. It may well be that God created Human Beings with their unpredictability and their human foibles for his own amusements. I feel that my stories are much more entertaining for the reader when I add some unexpected humour, or at least some snide comments which they can relate to, because they have lived it too.

I write because I have to love write, and I write to get the ideas out of my head and onto the page and are now visible on the page, and not just a figment of my imagination.

Writing undresses a writer, in what he has written. No fig leaf for modesty; more honest, more exposed than originally intended, often before unworthy eyes, including critics. To write something truly worth reading takes dedication and discipline. You have to adhere to personal honesty and honour within yourself to higher standards so as not to rob your own talent. Exactly how that concept manifests itself is up to each individual writer, if they actually strive to create real art, real literature, to know that they have lived up to the true full potential of their talent.

With your background in television, do you envision any of your stories, perhaps A Love To Die For, being adapted into a film or TV series? If so, how do you think the visual medium might enhance your storytelling?

I truly do believe that A Love To Die For would make a wonderful, timeless classic movie about life, the power of love in spite of the loss of true love, the feelings about powerlessness, and the Human Spirit's ability to change things and overcome the problem which life puts before us. Grace has amazing, strong, loving girlfriends whose strength of love carry her along when she gives up. They move her forward and work to get her back on her own two feet to persist in creating a new life for herself and her fatherless children. The love of her girlfriends forms the foundation upon which she can build her new life. And to evolve to a place where she can teach others what she has learned, and therefore elevate their lives.

There are some thematic similarities to the classic movie, "It's a wonderful life." So maybe A Love To Die For can someday become that type of timeless classic movie with an uplifting story.

PHOTO: Dr. Adebola Ajao, senior epidemiologist, author, and empowerment advocate, shares insights on career growth and work-life balance.

Empowers Professional Women
ADEBOLA AJAO
Insights, Strategies, and Inspiration for Thriving in Career and Life

Dr. Adebola Ajao is a force to be reckoned with. A senior epidemiologist, accomplished author, dynamic keynote speaker, and devoted wife and mother, she embodies the essence of empowerment in every facet of her life. With over two decades of experience in public health research, Dr. Ajao is not only dedicated to advancing women's health but also to guiding professional women towards unlocking their full potential.

Her journey is one marked by resilience and a relentless pursuit

Dr. Adebola Ajao shares her journey, empowering principles, mentorship insights, and practical advice for professional women striving to balance career and family.

of growth. Armed with a Doctor of Philosophy degree in molecular epidemiology, a master's degree in public health, and a Bachelor of Science in Biology, with a minor in Psychology, Dr. Ajao has navigated the complexities of academia and the professional world with grace and determination. Yet, it was during a period of internal struggle

that she found her true calling: empowering women to transcend limitations and embrace their greatness.

Dr. Ajao's commitment to empowerment is palpable in everything she does. As the founder of empowering initiatives, she has created a platform where professional women can harness their passion,

embrace personal development, and serve humanity with purpose. Her debut book, *Empowered Woman*, is a testament to her mission, offering practical insights and transformative principles to help women unlock their potential and thrive in their careers and personal lives.

In her speaking engagements, workshops, and coaching programs, Dr. Ajao imparts invaluable wisdom drawn from her own journey. She emphasizes five growth principles—Thinking Big, Conquering Your Fears, Seeking and Acquiring Knowledge, Finding Mentors, and Acting and Following Through—as

Empowered Woman and The Habits Code by Dr. Adebola Ajao, offering transformative wisdom for professional women navigating their careers.

the cornerstone of empowerment for professional women. Through these principles, she equips women with the tools they need to cultivate a growth mindset, embrace their strengths, and chart a course towards success.

However, Dr. Ajao's impact extends beyond the podium. As a mentor and advocate, she understands the critical role that mentorship plays in the journey of professional women. She emphasizes the importance of finding the right mentors and cultivating meaningful relationships that foster growth, support, and opportunity.

Yet, Dr. Ajao's insights are not merely theoretical—they are rooted in her own experiences as a professional, wife, and mother of three. She understands the challenges of balancing career aspirations with family responsibilities firsthand. Her advice is grounded in practical wisdom, encouraging women to prioritize their values, set realistic goals, establish healthy routines, delegate responsibilities, and prioritize self-care.

In a world where the journey of professional women is often fraught with obstacles, Dr. Adebola Ajao stands as a beacon of hope and empowerment. Through her words, actions, and unwavering commitment, she continues to inspire women to rise above adversity, embrace their

> Dr. Adebola Ajao's empowering journey and principles inspire women to embrace their potential and thrive in both career and life.

potential, and rewrite the narrative of their lives.

What inspired you to write *Empowered Woman* and focus on empowering professional women?

In my post-doctoral career, I landed a dream job as an epidemiologist at a highly prestigious federal agency. However, many years into my career, I was feeling stretched, stuck, stagnant, and unfulfilled with no understanding of how to navigate my career growth as a minority female scientist, wife, and mother of three and no female mentors to guide me. This period of internal struggle was pivotal in my personal development and career growth. During this period, I came to realize that even though I was highly educated, I did not have the necessary tools to move to my next levels in my life and career. This period of navigating my career path was a pivotal time that taught me the power personal development, leaning into my strengths, redefining mentorship, growing my community, and the importance of service in reaching my potential and finding fulfillment. From this experience, I wrote and publish my first book *Empowered Woman* in 2021. This book is a culmination of the principles and lessons I learned in my journey as a female professional. I focused on inspiring professional women because as a professional woman, I did not have a female mentor who had successfully navigated a successful career and motherhood to give me the tools to advance my career while raising my three children. I believe that it is imperative for women to see other women in positions where they aim to be.

How do you believe the principles outlined in your book can specifically benefit professional women in their careers and personal lives?

The five principles outlined in the book are the basic growth requirements for reaching one's potential as a professional woman. The empowering principles when practiced consistently allows a woman to develop a growth mindset that is focused on vision, innovation, and progress to grow in their career and create a life of purpose. These principles empower women to discover their strengths, define their professional goals, take more risks, and consistently step up to their next professional challenge increasing their confidence, success, and impact.

As a keynote speaker, what are some common challenges you observe among professional women, and how do you address them in your presentations?

As a keynote speaker, one common challenge I see among professional women is that women are not thriving in their careers. Most professional women see their career as a job and a means to a paycheck and they no longer see their career as a calling or serving their life's purpose. Another common challenge is that most professional women who love what they do and are advancing get burned out quickly from overworking to prove themselves and feel their impact. This was where I was in my career so I can relate to both challenges. I address these challenges by teaching self-discovery, mindset shift, and practical action tools.

In your experience, what role do mentors play in the journey of professional women, and how can they effectively find and cultivate mentorship relationships?

Female mentors play a fundamental role in women's professional journey. Mentors can be an advisor, advocate, or sponsor. Professional women must identify key areas they want to grow in order to identify a mentor that can support their area of desired growth. Mentors and mentees must be appropriately matched, and expectations and deliverables must be clearly communicated upfront. Peers and community are also important for support, motivation, accountability, and opportunity for growth and visibility. All of these relationships should be cultivated and nurtured.

What advice would you give to professional women who are struggling to balance their career aspirations with family responsibilities, based on your own experiences as a professional, wife, and mother of three?

Balancing career aspirations with family responsibility is a huge challenge. My first advice would be to know your values and prioritize what is important to you including family, career, business, and self-care. Second, set realistic goals and timelines so the different areas of life can be nurtured to the extend necessary. Third, create healthy daily routines to improve predictability, time management, and prevents chaos. Fourth, delegate responsibilities that can be outsourced to free up time for important goals. Firth, prioritize self-care. Every woman must define what self-care means to her and incorporate into their daily routine.

A Tapestry of Change and Creativity
BRIAN HATHAWAY

From Financial Analyst to Bestselling Author: The Diverse Journey of a Literary Chameleon

Brian Hathaway discusses his eclectic past, acting influences, and dog-inspired bestseller, Hope For The Hounds, amidst a career interwoven with personal growth and creative evolution.

Amid the cacophony of modern literature, where voices clamour for attention with the urgency of breaking news, Brian Hathaway's story emerges with an unassuming gravity. A man whose life reads like a map crisscrossed with the lines of constant movement and change, Hathaway brings to the literary world a richness born from a tapestry of diverse experiences.

Brian Hathaway's journey is as colourful and varied as the characters he creates. From the fluctuating landscapes of finance to the wild frontiers of the dot-com era, from the creative hustle of digital marketing and PR to the dynamic world of Creative & Marketing staffing, Hathaway has navigated through a sea of careers. Yet, amidst these professional transformations, his passion for the arts remained a constant beacon. His seven-year tenure in the realms of acting and improv in New York City bestowed upon him an invaluable acumen for narrative and character that now infuses his written work.

His literary debut, *Hope For The Hounds*, has already etched its mark on readers, captivating them with a best-selling middle-grade urban fantasy that paints a futuristic New York City in broad, imaginative strokes. Dogs are not mere pets in this tale but pivotal societal pillars, reflecting Hathaway's own adoration for canine companions. The inspiration, he reveals, sprouted from a dream so vivid it propelled him from slumber to scribe.

The narrative tapestry grows more intricate with *COOPED UP*, Hathaway's sophomore novel that knits together the threads of family sagas and romantic comedies, all while delving into the profound themes of politics, social justice, and relationships. It is a story shaped by the personal trials of a global pandemic and the intimate struggle against illness within his family, told with an authenticity that can only come from lived experience.

In conversation with Reader's House Magazine, Hathaway opens up about his inspirations, his process, and his aspirations. He discusses how his acting background lends itself to crafting vivid characters and engaging dialogue, how personal tribulations have informed his narratives, and how he plans to leverage his entertainment industry savvy to connect with readers in an ever-evolving publishing landscape.

As Brian Hathaway stands on the cusp of new creative horizons, exploring potential projects that range from heroic wartime tales to gripping true crime, one thing remains certain: his voice—a harmonious blend of humour and heartache, realism and hope—resonates with a clarity that speaks to the resilience of the human spirit. Join us as we delve into the world of an author who embodies the very essence of transformation, whose stories remind us that stability isn't about standing still—it's about finding your anchor in the tumultuous sea of life.

Hope For The Hounds - Unleash the adventure where canines lead and human bonds are tested.

Your debut novel, *Hope For The Hounds*, offers readers a fascinating glimpse into a futuristic New York City where dogs have become integral members of society. What inspired you to create this imaginative world, and how did your own experiences with dogs influence the story?

I knew I wanted to write a story - I just couldn't commit to an idea or even genre. Was it going to be Sci-Fi? Fantasy? Rom-Com? Superheroes? My wife gave me a copy of Julia Cameron's The Artist's Way, and in diligently working on the program, I had an epiphany in the form of a powerful dream. I dreamt that our bulldog saved my wife from an apartment fire by flying her out a window and landing her to safety on the city street below. When I woke up, I started writing that day. It combines urban fantasy with science fiction and in this case, the superheroes are the dogs.

I've always loved dogs so in my story, they're the ensemble cast of characters told through the perspective of Hope, a 12-year-old girl, and her best friend, Keely, an American bulldog.

In *Cooped Up*, you blend elements of romantic comedy with poignant themes of family, struggle, and resilience. Can you share more about the inspiration behind this novel and how your background in acting and comedy shaped the narrative?

My ideas seem to come when I'm searching for my next book. I'm two for two anyway. In this case, it was March of 2020, I had the idea of a stand-up comedian who was going on a national tour but he brings his Mom with him once she's been diagnosed with terminal cancer and given a year to live. Then real-life smacked me in the face in the form of a global pandemic and my Mom was diagnosed with bladder cancer that summer. I shifted my idea to writing in real time about the pandemic while figuring out what a comedy tour in the Fall of 2020 would look like. In my research, I chatted with one of my best friends, who's been a stand-up comedian for twenty years. I took my Mom's journey with cancer and incorporated it into the story. So although this is a fictional story, there's truth on every page. I admire comedians so much and for me, it's the truest form of art. It's the only artform that is a real-time interaction with the performer and the audience. I've always loved making people laugh, so that was a main motivation in writing this book.

Your journey from acting and improv in New York City to becoming a writer is quite unique. How did your experiences in the entertainment industry inform your writing process, particularly when it comes to crafting engaging characters and dialogue?

I write visually. I see the movie in my mind as I write. My goal with both my books and the ones coming after is to see them as a TV series or movie.

My training in character development and Improv lends credence to my work because I can peel back the layers of characters like an onion. I try to write realistic dialogue so that each character comes with their own, unique perspectives. For me, the most interesting characters are the sympathetic bad guys and flawed heroes. After all, everyone is the hero of their own story.

Cooped Up tackles timely themes of family, illness, and the impact of the global pandemic, offering a heartfelt exploration of love and resilience. How did your personal experiences, such as caring for your mother during her chemotherapy, influence the themes and emotions portrayed in the book?

First of all, I couldn't believe it when my mom told me she had cancer (again) after I started writing Cooped Up. So her bladder cancer and her journey with it is documented in the book. Ultimately, I wanted this book to be about hope because we had just lived through a global pandemic and I felt everyone needed something to cling to that gives them a sense of good in this world. Although these are heavy topics, I didn't want the book to be misery porn either. I want realism mixed with laugh-out-loud moments and a happy ending. No spoilers though!

I've very recently updated the timeline of Cooped Up to take place this year, in the Fall of 2024. I feel it brings a bit more timeliness and relevance to the story. I'm amazed how similar things are in 2024 as they were in 2020.

With your background in entertainment and PR, you bring a unique perspective to the publishing world. How do you envision leveraging your industry connections and experiences to promote your books and connect with readers?

I decided to self-publish Hope For The Hounds and after that valuable learning experience, I'm waiting for an agent to represent me to pitch Cooped Up to traditional publishers.

I have friends in entertainment who I think will help me promote my book when it comes out. I'm thinking of morning talk shows and late-night talk shows. I also believe a tv/film deal may come along with the publishing deal. I'll be cashing in ll of my favors for sure!

Looking ahead, what other creative projects or writing endeavors are you currently exploring? Are there any genres or themes you're excited to explore in future works or any particular storytelling techniques you hope to further develop in your writing journey?

Great question! It's one I've been wrestling with recently. I've been speaking with my old high school buddy whose grandfather was in all these famous battles of WWII. His grandfather is like the Forest Gump of WWII. I'm thinking of writing a fictionalized version of his grandpa's story.

I've also spoken with another friend who's a New York City police detective and he was telling me about this case of his. It's mindblowing and he wants to turn it into a book after he retires in a couple of years. I can see myself getting involved in that one too.

So the two themes that I seem to be gravitating towards are true stories of heroism and true crime.

Of course, I've been thinking about the sequels to Hope For The Hounds and Cooped Up too!

PHOTO: A master storyteller, Brian Hathaway transforms life's chaos into literary magic, capturing hearts with his imaginative and relatable narratives.

PHOTO: *KM Taylor's mastery of blending historical settings with supernatural elements is unparalleled, captivating readers with every turn of the page.*

A Journey into the Worlds of
KM TAYLOR
Exploring Themes of Light, Dark, and the Supernatural with an Emerging Literary Voice

KM Taylor discusses inspirations, world-building from dreams, and character complexities, blending history with the supernatural in her genre-bending works.

KM Taylor, a multifaceted artist, veteran writer, and burgeoning author, is carving her niche in the literary world with an electrifying fusion of horror, fantasy, and the supernatural. With her debut novel, *Codex Sohrakia: The Gifted Dark,* earning accolades and her sophomore effort, *The Devil's Conquest,* captivating readers with its blend of romance and adventure, Taylor's imaginative prowess knows no bounds.

In her interview with Reader's House Magazine, Taylor offers insights into her creative process, revealing the profound inspirations that drive her narratives. Drawing from a rich tapestry of influences spanning philosophy, dreams, and real-life experiences, she intricately weaves together themes of creation, order, and chaos, inviting readers into worlds both hauntingly familiar and tantalizingly exotic.

Taylor's ability to craft immersive worlds, born from the depths of her lucid dreams, breathes life into her stories, infusing them with a palpable sense of wonder and mystery. Whether navigating the treacherous seas alongside pirates or unravelling the enigmatic forces of light and darkness, her characters grapple with complex ethical choices, mirroring the intricacies of the human psyche.

Influenced by a diverse array of creators, from literary giants like Anne Rice and H.P. Lovecraft to visionary manga artists Tite Kubo and Akira Toriyama, Taylor's work stands as a testament to the transformative power of storytelling. With each page, she challenges conventions, redefining the boundaries of genre and imagination.

As she continues to embark on her literary odyssey, Taylor remains steadfast in her commitment to authenticity and innovation, seamlessly blending historical settings with supernatural elements to create narratives that resonate deeply with readers. With a boundless imagination and an unwavering passion for storytelling, she invites us to journey with her into the realms of darkness and light, where the lines between reality and fantasy blur, and the possibilities are as endless as the stars in the night sky.

Your debut novel, Codex Sohrakia: The Gifted Dark,

KM Taylor, author of Codex Sohrakia: The Gifted Dark and The Devil's Conquest, shares insights into her creative process.

delves into complex themes of creation, order, and chaos. What inspired you to explore such profound concepts in your writing?

The initial concept came to me as I was reading various non-fiction books on world philosophies. I've always had a fascination with concepts of deity and spirituality, so I wanted to explore new perspectives based on age-old dogmas, and with an unexpected approach.

The world-building in Codex Sohrakia is intricate and immersive, spanning realms of light and darkness. Can you share more about your process for developing these fantastical worlds and their underlying mythologies?

Most details come directly from my lucid dreams. All my life I've dreamed wild and interesting things. There are some instances within the book that come straight out of my dream journal..

The Devil's Conquest takes readers on a romantic and thrilling adventure with pirates and a supernatural twist. What drew you to the pirate genre, and how do you approach infusing it with elements of the supernatural?

Classic pirates have always fascinated me. My father was a navy man. He loved all things nautical! A large framed print of a massive galleon hung over his desk. I loved staring at it as I daydreamed. I also loved the Pirates of the Caribbean ride at Disney, which certainly was an influence. The germ that evolved into The Devil's Conquest came from the documentary Blackbeard: Terror at Sea. Regarding the supernatural elements. Well, they seemed appropriate, simply because there are many mysterious legends in pirate lore. Plus, I prefer to write fantastical things and felt it enriched the story, providing a nice, epic climax.

In both of your novels, there's a strong interplay between light and darkness, order and chaos. How do these opposing forces influence your characters and drive the narrative forward?

I have a propensity for duality in my interests, as well as in my creations. It's a trope I love to explore and do unique things with. Good and evil, as concepts, are used often. But typically creators follow expected tropes. I like to play with the idea that light & dark, good & evil may not be what we perceive them to be. That is a core concept of Codex Sohrakia.

Your writing showcases a deep exploration of characters' inner struggles and moral dilemmas. How do you approach character development, particularly when dealing with protagonists facing complex ethical choices?

Psychology has always interested me, and I enjoy dealing with inner struggles that influence character's actions, and the resulting effects of those actions. Finding the emotion and the drive for each character comes from my own personal experiences. I apply mundane struggles to my strange worlds and heightened situations, amplifying them to serve the dramatics of each tale. I work on every scene until I feel them, knowing that, if I am moved as I write, then the reader will, hopefully, also be moved.

As a writer who navigates both fantasy and historical fiction genres, what challenges do you encounter when blending elements of the supernatural with historical settings, and how do you ensure authenticity while still allowing for imaginative storytelling?

I honestly have not found it difficult merging supernatural elements into historical fiction. Magic and the unexplained are as old as time. The most important thing is to gain a sense of the times and places. I set aside modern sensibilities. For The Devil's Conquest, I immersed myself in pirate lore, read and watched documentaries, which helped me to feel for each character in their respective settings.

Are there any specific creators that influence your works? Who, or what, inspires you and gets your creative juices flowing?

There are several authors/creators who have inspired my work. My best friend, RL Davis Hays, with whom I wrote stories back in high school (she has published several wonderful books). Anne Rice's The Vampire Chronicles, specifically. HP Lovecraft, his poetic style and the creepiness of his descriptions, enthrals me. Then, I discovered the British horror author, Brian Lumley. His Necroscope series blew my mind and sent my writing off into entirely new dimensions! I must also give credit to two of my favourite Japanese mangaka: Tite Kubo and Akira Toriyama, whose fierce imaginations help me not to box myself in creatively.

> KM Taylor's imaginative prowess crafts intricate worlds, delving into the depths of human nature with compelling characters and narratives.

Crafting Worlds of Dark Fantasy and Moral Ambiguity
R.C. VIELEE
Exploring Morality, Parallel Realities, and the Power of Imagination in Utopia Falling

Award-winning author R.C. Vielee discusses inspirations, moral complexities, and thematic depth in Utopia Falling: A Darkness Rises in an exclusive interview.

Delving into the depths of imagination and moral complexity, R.C. Vielee stands as a luminary in the realm of dark fantasy fiction. With a notable debut novel, *Utopia Falling: A Darkness Rises,* Vielee has captivated readers with a narrative that transcends mere storytelling, delving into the very essence of human nature and societal constructs.

Vielee's journey from the quiet landscapes of northern New Jersey to the intricate tapestry of his literary creations is a testament to his multifaceted talent. Before wielding the pen as an award-winning author, Vielee honed his craft through the lens of a camera, capturing the beauty of the natural world as a landscape photographer. Yet, beneath the surface of serene landscapes lies a mind deeply intrigued by the mysteries of astrophysics, hinting at the vast expanse of his creative horizon.

In a recent interview with Reader's House Magazine, Vielee opens the door to the worlds he has meticulously crafted, shedding light on the inspirations and complexities that permeate his work. At the heart of his narrative lies the dichotomy between Tartica and Evidar, two realms steeped in contrasting ideologies and moral quandaries. Reflecting on the tumultuous state of our own world, Vielee draws parallels between the struggles of his fictional realms and the divisive realities we face today.

Central to *Utopia Falling*f is the theme of parallel realities, where individual actions reverberate across dimensions, shaping the fate of entire civilizations. Through characters like Reyne, Vielee navigates the intricate web of personal desires and societal obligations, challenging readers to confront the blurred lines between right and wrong.

Yet, it is in the moral ambiguity of characters like Neladith and the enigmatic Devil's Blacksmith that Vielee truly shines. By crafting individuals grappling with their own desires and loyalties, he invites readers to introspect on the complexities of human nature, transcending the boundaries of hero and villain.

As readers journey through the pages of *Utopia Falling,* they are confronted with themes of redemption, power, and the resilience of the human spirit. Vielee's narrative resonates with the raw emotions

Dive into the immersive world of 'Utopia Falling: A Darkness Rises' by R.C. Vielee, where parallel realities and moral ambiguity collide.

of grief, sorrow, and loss, yet amidst the darkness, a glimmer of hope emerges. Through the trials and tribulations of his characters, Vielee imparts a profound message of resilience and the enduring power of the human spirit to triumph over adversity.

In Vielee's worlds, darkness and light intertwine, painting a vivid portrait of the human experience. As readers embark on this immersive journey, they are beckoned to confront their own beliefs, challenging preconceived notions and embracing the complexities that define us all.

What inspired you to create the world of Tartica and Evidar, and how did you go about developing their contrasting societies?

The state of our world today inspired me to create the realms of Tartica and Evidar. Tartica is seen as a near-utopia by its people, whereas Evidar is a brutal, violent place, forever in darkness.

Like the fantasy world created in Utopia Falling, in society today individuals at opposite ends of the political spectrum, or people holding different religious beliefs, and even those who disagree on climate science all share a common thread; the fervent amongst them vehemently believes the other side is not only wrong but are in the dark.

In Utopia Falling the story centers on Tartica's fight for survival. Yet, the underlying threat to Tartica is Evidar's quest for salvation at the expense of Tartica's ruination. It begs the question; how does one

> R.C. Vielee's Utopia Falling immerses readers in a world of dark fantasy, offering a gripping narrative that challenges and captivates.

interpret absolute morality if the worldview that one civilization holds, conflicts with the worldview of another? Are some issues of morality beyond question, while others are not? Can one overarching concept of morality be absolute? In writing Utopia Falling I didn't take sides. I left it for the reader to interpret, or for the reader to ignore these larger issues and just lose themselves in a great fantasy story.

The theme of parallel realities and the consequences of individual actions seem to be central to *Utopia Falling: A Darkness Rises.* **Could you elaborate on how this theme influenced the plot and character development?**

Whether you live in the UK, the USA, or anywhere else, one's perspective can be influenced by their socioeconomic conditions, political affiliations, race, religion, and so much more. People living in the same country, the same town, the same village, often hold different perceptions of it. It can seem like individuals living in society come from different worlds. In Utopia Falling, Earth exists in different dimensions composed of people originating from the same point of origin. The experience of living in one dimension or the other sets each character on a path to take actions they believe best serves their realm.

Reyne's internal conflict between his personal desires and the larger fate of Tartica is compelling. How did you approach crafting his character arc, particularly in navigating his relationships and moral dilemmas?

In Utopia Falling the main character, Reyne, is an everyman. He wants to reap the promise of society engrained in the social contract: that if you play by the rules, you get the rewards. He quickly finds out that the little guy (or gal) is but a pawn in a game played by more powerful forces. The social contract serves the general population until it conflicts with the desires of the power brokers who play by different rules. Reyne is pressed to abandon his own self-interest–to marry the woman he loves, for the benefit of civilization's 'greater good'. His internal struggle is a metaphor for questioning the obligation of abiding by the demands of the greater good when the greater good breaks the promises inherent in its social contract.

The character Neladith serves as an antagonist but also seems to grapple with her own desires and loyalties. Can you discuss the complexities of creating characters who are morally ambiguous and the role they play in your narrative?

Each of us has issues with moral ambiguities when our self-interest comes into conflict with acceptable norms. It happens in everyday life more often than we care to admit. There's a part of ourselves we hide from others. Sometimes it's driven by desires that don't fit in with what everyone else wants or what everyone else is doing. The hard wiring in our caveman brains tells us there is safety in the group and to subvert our self-centered wants in exchange for acceptance.

In Utopia Falling, I explore that aspect of the human condition through several characters, whether they are the good guys or the bad guys. Neladith is certainly a character you can love to hate. Her internal struggle tells us that self-interest is something even the bad guys have to resolve. Underneath it all, we're all the same, wherever we come from.

The concept of the Devil's Blacksmith and his manipulation of events adds an intriguing layer of political intrigue to the story. What inspired this character, and how did you develop the dynamics between him and other key figures like Jerithan?

In Utopia Falling, the Devil's Blacksmith is the incarnation of the unseen forces that shape our world, whether that's on a global basis or on the smaller scale of interpersonal relationships. To some the Devil's Blacksmith might represent the deep state directing political actors to do their bidding. In the case of Jerithan, the Voice he hears in his thoughts prods him to take actions that ultimately serve the Devil's Blacksmith's objectives disguised in the offerings of something Jerithan desires.

Utopia Falling: A Darkness Rises **blends elements of dark fantasy with themes of redemption and the consequences of power. How do you see these themes resonating with readers, and what messages or emotions do you hope they take away from the book?**

Utopia Falling's dark fantasy theme, verging on grimdark, is intended to hold a mirror up to the realities of life. Everyone faces difficult challenges. Sometimes we can rise above them. Others push us to our limits. And there are struggles we cannot overcome. We are defined by how we deal with tragedy. Some become bitter. Others become resentful. But the lucky can absorb the blow and become better for having successfully faced it head on. The joy we experience in life is so often influenced by how well each of us deals with the inevitable hardships each of us must face.

Utopia Falling will touch your emotions as you experience life through the eyes of the various characters. Grief, sorrow, and loss certainly play a role, but there is always hope. Like each of us in our own lives, the characters in Utopia Falling just have to find it.

PHOTO: *Denise Alicea, author of diverse genres, shares her journey from Manhattan to Connecticut, blending personal experiences with creative storytelling.*

Exploring Infinite Worlds with
DENISE ALICEA
A Conversation on Writing Across Genres and Emotional Storytelling

Denise Alicea discusses her multi-genre writing approach, inspirations from personal experiences, and advice for aspiring authors in this insightful interview.

Denise Alicea's journey as a writer began in the bustling heart of Manhattan, New York, and continued through the serene landscapes of Connecticut. Her creative spirit found its first expression in drawing and painting, but it was through the written word that she truly discovered her voice. Denise's literary career blossomed at the tender age of fifteen with her initial foray into poetry, which set the stage for a rich and diverse exploration of genres including fantasy, time travel, action, adventure, and romance.

As an esteemed member of the Romance Writers of America since 2005, Denise has not only garnered accolades for her short stories but also consistently contributed to the writing community through her book review blog, The Pen & Muse Book Reviews. Her commitment to the craft is evident in her dedication to both her personal writing and her efforts to support and mentor fellow authors.

In our interview, Denise shares insights into her multifaceted writing process, discussing how she meticulously researches each genre to ensure authenticity and depth. From her poignant poetry in *Heartbeats in Ink* to the emotionally charged narrative of *Consoling Angel*, and the historical richness of *Destined ~ A Time Travel Romance Anthology*, Denise reveals the intricate layers of her storytelling. She also delves into her latest work, *Angels Always Near: A Poetry Collection*, offering a reflective look at teenage emotions through a mature lens.

Denise's words are a testament to the power of storytelling and the importance of perseverance, providing invaluable advice for aspiring writers eager to explore various genres and discover their unique voice. Her ability to weave personal experiences into her fiction and poetry creates a profound connection with her readers, making her stories not just tales of imagination, but heartfelt journeys of love, loss, and self-discovery.

Denise, your diverse background in writing spans fantasy, time travel, romance, and more. What draws you to explore such varied genres, and how do you approach

each genre differently in your writing process?

I approach each genre differently with lots of research! I find that reading in the genre and doing research really does help write in different genres. I also love to explore different genres because I love learning new things. I'm also a reader who loves a variety of different genres.

Heartbeats in Ink is described as a rollercoaster ride through the highs and lows of love and life. Can you share some insights into your inspiration behind this collection of heartfelt poetry, and how your personal experiences influence your writing in this anthology?

All the poetry that I have written has some emotional tie to me, family or a friend that has gone through it whether it's falling in love, a crush, or even the lows of being alone, etc. I think people forget that love always brings a variety of emotions and feeling, not all of them being flowery. Growing up I found it easier to express my feelings via paper then in person, it grew into a collection of poetry book that I still have and draw inspiration for new poems.

Consoling Angel follows Mira, who finds solace in her admiration for the Hollywood actor James Dean. What inspired you to blend elements of grief, admiration, and wish fulfillment in this romance story, and how do you create emotional depth in your characters?

Consoling Angel was a short story close to my heart, as it's a first short story where I could take the grief of losing someone you love, adding a romance story, but adding a young woman finding comfort in someone. The inspiration came from having a great admiration for the actor James Dean. I have personally lost some family and friends; and know that grief is not an easy subject to deal with. I think personally when someone we love passes, you always have those *"what if"* moments. I create emotional depth by really describing what that character is going through and not being a friend to express it via dialogue or show what they're feeling via body language.

Destined ~ A Time Travel Romance Anthology features stories set in various historical periods, including 1950s New York and war-torn 387 BC Ireland. What challenges and joys did you encounter while crafting these time-travel narratives, and how do you balance historical accuracy with imaginative storytelling?

I was fortunate to write this anthology with a fellow author and friend. The challenges that you face when writing a time travel romance are the keeping the time periods straight and trying to keep the accuracy of the any historical events. I would have to say the joys were telling the stories of these couples and of course worldbuilding.

How do you balance historical accuracy with imaginative storytelling? Research! The storytelling is important, but as long as I get the broad strokes of the historical accuracy right, avoid glaring anachronisms, I find that it mostly just fits together. The research is important to make sure I don't write something completely off the period, but other than that, tell the story first, then fact check it.

Angels Always Near: A Poetry Collection offers an experimental exploration of adolescence and love, filtered through a mature adult perspective. How do you navigate the complexities of teenage emotions and ideals in your poetry, and what themes do you hope readers will resonate with in this collection?

Angels Always Near was my first poetry book where I took my own teenage poems and translated them now being older. So, all the feelings I felt over 30 years ago I wrote down at the time I was feeling them. Translating them and rewriting portions really helped me look back at what I was going through. I hope readers can resonate with the emotions of feeling love, friendship, and of course a little bit of anger and frustration. All emotions that not only teenagers face these days.

As a writer who has won awards for your short stories and received recognition for your diverse writing, what advice do you have for aspiring authors looking to explore multiple genres and find their unique voice in writing?

My advice for all aspiring writers is to constantly read, read the genres you are writing, read craft books, and join writing groups where you can share your work. Writing can be lonely, but it doesn't have to be. I have great groups that I am a part of that I love meeting with even if its once a month.

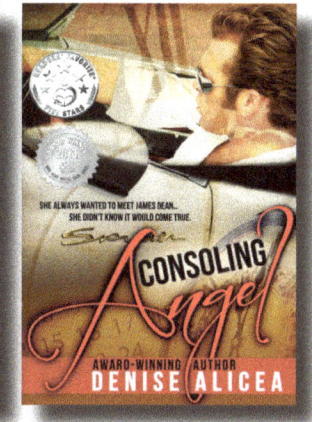

A captivating collection of Denise Alicea's works, showcasing her versatility in poetry, romance, fantasy, and time travel.

Denise Alicea masterfully blends emotional depth and imaginative storytelling, making her a standout in diverse literary genres.

PHOTO: *Author Michèle Olson brings the magic of Mackinac Island to life in her captivating novels filled with mystery, romance, and faith.*

Unveiling Mackinac Mysteries
MICHÈLE OLSON
Crafting Diverse Characters and Captivating Stories

BY DAN PETERS

Michèle Olson discusses her Mackinac Island Stories series, blending mystery, romance, and faith, crafting diverse characters against the backdrop of this unique locale.

Michèle Olson's creative journey spans over four decades, encompassing advertising, marketing, broadcasting, and now, fiction writing. With a professional voice career that includes DJing during the era of records, Michèle has ventured into the realm of storytelling with her Mackinac Island Stories series. Inspired by her love for the enchanting *Mackinac Island in Michigan*, Michèle brings to life tales of mystery, romance, friendship, and faith against the backdrop of this unique locale.

The allure of *Mackinac Island*, with its prohibition on cars and reliance on horses and bikes for transportation, serves as more than just a picturesque setting. It becomes a character in itself, influencing the narrative and shaping the lives of Michèle's protagonists. For Michèle, the island holds a special place in her heart, having frequented it for over 40 years. Through her novels, she invites readers to experience the island's beauty and charm, even when they can't be there in person.

In each installment of her series, Michèle introduces readers to a new protagonist facing their own set of challenges and mysteries. From the vibrant Piper Penn to the titular characters like Ethel, Dorothy, Alice, Wendy, and Nancy, Michèle crafts diverse characters spanning different professions, personalities, and ages. Through their journeys, readers encounter themes of mystery, mayhem, mirth, and miracles, finding pieces of themselves mirrored in these fictional lives.

What sets Michèle's novels apart is the seamless integration of diverse genres—mystery, romance, and faith. Striking a balance between these elements while maintaining a cohesive narrative poses its challenges, but Michèle navigates them skillfully. Her stories explore faith not as a separate entity, but as an integral part of her characters' lives, guiding them through difficult decisions and life choices.

Beyond writing, Michèle's other creative pursuits—broadcasting, voice work, and sketchdoodling—influence her approach to storytelling. These diverse mediums converge under her creative imprint, Lake Girl Publishing, blurring the lines between imagination and reality. Drawing from her own experiences and interests, Michèle infuses authenticity into her characters and settings, ensuring they resonate with readers on a personal level.

At the heart of Michèle's storytelling lies a message of self-acceptance and embracing one's true self in a world that often overlooks individuals. Through her narratives, she reminds readers of their inherent worth and uniqueness, echoing the message of love and acceptance found in timeless stories and parables. Ultimately, Michèle's hope is that her readers, amidst laughter, tears, and wonder, find themselves reflected in the pages of her novels, embracing their own stories with newfound acceptance and joy.

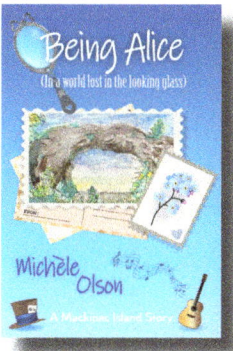

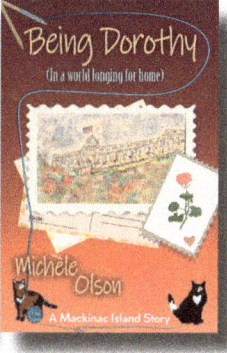
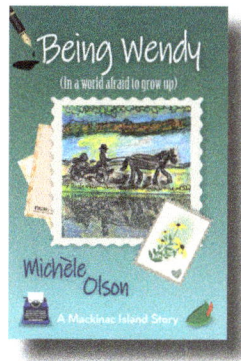

Step into the world of Michèle Olson's Mackinac Island Stories series, where mysteries unfold against the backdrop of this enchanting locale.

Your Mackinac Island Stories series explores themes of mystery, romance, friendship, and faith against the backdrop of Mackinac Island. What inspired you to set your stories in this particular location, and how does the island itself influence the narrative and characters?

Mackinac Island is a very unique, real place located where the upper peninsula and lower peninsula of the state of Michigan meet. To this day, there are no cars allowed. The transportation is horses and bikes. It is where Lake Michigan and Lake Huron meet, in a body of water called the Straits of Mackinac. The shops, houses, and the famous Grand Hotel, along with the lush seasonal environment truly makes it a place that is Somewhere in Time. (The name of the movie shot there in 1979 with Christopher Reeve and Jane Seymour). My husband and I live about five hours away in Wisconsin, and we've been going to the island for over 40 years. That made it the perfect place to set my stories. Although there are year-round residents, the population swells in spring, summer, and fall when a million people go to see the beauty of the area. As a mystery writer, it makes it a perfect place for people to hide and go incognito! I love it very much, so writing my novels set there lets me feel like I'm at the Grand Hotel and the island. Readers tell me they feel the same. It's a way to be there when they can't be there in person.

Each installment in your series follows a different protagonist facing unique challenges and mysteries. How do you approach crafting these diverse characters, and what do you hope readers take away from their individual journeys?

While the books can be read as "stand alones" you can read them in order. Being Ethel (In a world that loves Lucy) starts in 1979. Being Dorothy (In a world longing for home) is 1980. Being Alice (In a world lost in the looking glass) is 1981. Being Wendy (In a world afraid to grow up) is 1982. And the latest, Being Nancy (In a world lost in mystery) is 1983. As a mystery writer, I didn't want the crimes and mysteries to be solvable with a cell phone! I like the era when we still had to go to a phone booth or send a telegram.

We meet Piper Penn in Being Ethel and understand her story. She continues on in every story but becomes someone that the protagonist in each of the other stories, meets. The new character become the focus. They are all very unique in their professions, personalities, and ages. The main characters run from ages 20's to 70s. They all encounter mystery, mayhem, mirth, and miracles. What I hope a reader takes away is seeing themselves in some aspect of each character's journey. I do have consistent side characters and a villain who shows up in each book…readers love that

Being Ethel, Being Dorothy, Being Alice, Being Wendy and now Being Nancy each feature strong female protagonists navigating complex situations. What inspired you to focus on these women's stories, and how do you ensure their experiences resonate with readers?

People love the titles, and it's an instant connection for the reader. Ethel and Lucy, Dorothy resonates with Wizard of Oz, Alice – Alice in Wonderland, Wendy-Peter Pan, and Nancy–Nancy Drew…they all lay the groundwork to explore the personality of the people coming to Mackinac Island, plus interweaving aspects of those stories that affect the female protagonist's lives. The latest Being Nancy book is for all those people who grew up reading Nancy Drew…so many of us! The lessons of the girl sleuth are woven into a Nancy Drew convention at the Grand Hotel in 1983.

Your novels blend elements of mystery, romance, and faith. How do you strike a balance between these genres while maintaining a cohesive narrative, and what challenges do you encounter in weaving together these different themes?

I find faith to be extremely important when it comes to life choices. That's what these ladies are facing through the stories – lots of life choices. I do get feedback from people who weren't looking for a story of faith woven into the mystery and mayhem. The feedback has been mostly positive. They get to see hard life questions play out in the lives of these characters. Sometimes, the questions are ones the readers have wondered about themselves. I think the stories are also interesting to someone who doesn't have a strong faith life, too. It's simply what happens to these characters and what they observe in the lives of those who have found peace in trying circumstances. It's their story, just as anyone reconciles life difficulties in their journey. Whether or not the reader finds it applies to their life is optional. But it's always food for thought.

The character of Sister Mary-Margaret in Being Ethel is beloved by readers. She is a fan favorite- I've received lots of feedback and love for that character.

In addition to writing, you're also a broadcaster, voice pro, and sketchdoodler. How do these diverse creative pursuits inform your approach to storytelling, and do you find that they influence each other in unexpected ways?

They all fall under my creative imprint: Lake Girl Publishing. The lines blur – my voicework helps me "hear" the characters, sketchdoodling is a help in seeing where the story goes. I do the art for all the postcards on the covers. In future stories, I'll be delving into my radio/TV background in the 70s, because that's a world I know. All the characters professions: artists, author, collector, musician, and Nancy Drew lover…are things I know and love. Except maybe the spy theme of Being Dorothy…I've never been a spy. Or have I? :)

Your message involves the importance of being seen, valued, and unique in a world that often overlooks individuals. How do you weave this message into your storytelling, and what do you hope readers take away from your books in terms of self-acceptance and embracing their true selves?

If you read the Bible, you will see parables and stories were an intricate part of teaching people how to love, share, and put others before themselves. We also see how God loves each of us, flaws and all, and would leave the 99 sheep to go after the one who is lost. That's an important message for each of us. We are loved, cared for, adored, and there is a plan for each of us to live an abundant life. I hope that comes through in every story. That's a pretty important message to embrace, the truth that goes beyond the fiction to the heart. Along the way we laugh, we cry, we wonder, and we learn. The ultimate story is when the reader puts their name after "Being".

PHOTO: *Cordell Parvin, esteemed legal coach and author, sharing his insights on career development and client acquisition.*

From Law Practice to Legal Coaching

CORDELL PARVIN

How One Lawyer's Transition to Coaching Transformed Careers and Inspired a Generation

Cordell Parvin transitioned from practicing construction law to coaching lawyers, focusing on career development, client acquisition, and personal fulfilment, significantly impacting over 1000 lawyers across the US and Canada.

Cordell Parvin is a name synonymous with legal career development, particularly within the spheres of client acquisition and professional growth for attorneys. With an extensive career spanning over three decades, Parvin's expertise in construction law transitioned seamlessly into a full-time dedication to coaching lawyers, a move fueled by his profound desire to contribute more meaningfully to the legal profession. His journey from a practicing attorney to a revered coach is marked by a distinct commitment to fostering the professional success and personal fulfillment of lawyers across the United States and Canada.

Parvin's extensive background includes not only his practice but also his influential roles as a speaker, writer, and blogger on career and client development. His presentations at numerous law firms and bar associations, coupled with his published works, have solidified his reputation as a thought leader in the legal industry. Parvin's coaching methodology is rooted in practical advice, emphasizing the importance of goal setting, time management, and maintaining a balance between professional obligations and personal life.

In his coaching career, which began in earnest in 2005, Parvin has imparted his knowledge to over 1000 lawyers from various firms, ranging from large, metropolitan practices to smaller, regional offices. His insights into common challenges faced by lawyers, such as time management for career and client development, are invaluable. Parvin advocates for a structured approach to professional growth, underscoring the significance of investing time in both career and personal development to achieve long-term success and fulfillment.

Through his books like *Say Ciao to Chow Mein: Conquering Career Burnout* and *Rising Star,* Parvin employs a storytelling approach inspired by Ken Blanchard. These parable-style narratives provide serious career advice in a relatable and engaging manner, addressing issues such as career burnout and the importance of balancing professional and personal life. Parvin's focus on practical solutions and personal anecdotes offers young lawyers

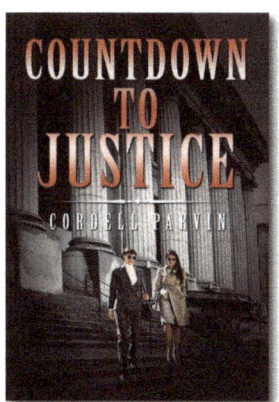
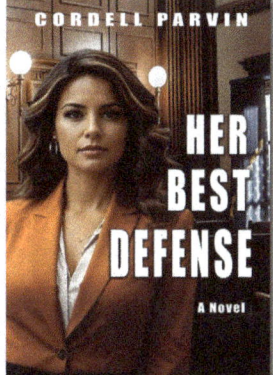

Cordell Parvin's influential books offer practical career advice and strategies for overcoming burnout, achieving balance, and becoming successful rainmakers.

guidance on navigating the complexities of a legal career while maintaining personal well-being.

Moreover, Parvin emphasizes the necessity of cultivating a collaborative culture within law firms. He identifies the inherent challenge in shifting from a competitive mindset, fostered early in legal education, to one that values teamwork and mentorship. His advice for fostering such a culture includes hiring lawyers with strong interpersonal skills, rewarding collaborative efforts, and prioritizing the development of junior lawyers.

For young lawyers aspiring to become successful rainmakers, Parvin's most crucial advice is to identify a compelling "*why*" behind their ambitions. This motivational cornerstone should drive the creation of comprehensive plans, spanning various timeframes, and instill the commitment and discipline required to follow through on these plans. His emphasis on a structured, disciplined approach to career development serves as a testament to his own successful transition from practicing lawyer to esteemed coach and mentor.

Cordell Parvin's wisdom and dedication have profoundly shaped the careers of countless lawyers, making him a beacon in legal coaching.

Your career spans from practicing law to becoming a well-known coach for lawyers. Can you share what motivated you to transition from practicing law to coaching, and what was the most rewarding aspect of this shift?

I practiced construction law for 38 years. All along the way I set goals and worked to achieve them. I represented some of the top contractors in the United States. In 2004 I had my best year. I was on top of my world and had exceeded goals I had set for myself. In that same year I coached brand new partners in my law firm. I felt more fulfilled helping those young lawyers. So, at the end of that year, I left my law practice to coach lawyers in the United States and Canada full-time. I gave up lots of money for feeling like I was making a greater contribution.

Say Ciao to Chow Mein: Conquering Career Burnout is a parable-style book that delivers serious career advice in a humorous manner. What inspired you to use this storytelling approach, and how do you think it enhances the message for young lawyers?

I got the idea from Ken Blanchard. Blanchard. His business parable books made sense to me. I wrote Say Ciao to Chow Mein: Conquering Career Burnout because I worked with young lawyers who were burning out. They were working very hard, but not enjoying their career. I wanted to help them deal with the challenges they were facing in their career and life.

You've coached over 1000 lawyers across diverse law firms. What are some common challenges you see lawyers face in client development, and what strategies do you recommend to overcome them?

One big challenge is making time for the activities that will make them successful and fulfilled. Young lawyers are typically doing work for older more experienced lawyers. and many don't think beyond the project they are working on for that lawyer.

I once wrote this: Suppose you sleep 8 hours a night, or 56 hours a week. Suppose you bill 40 hours a week and you invest another 10 hours a week on your career development, client development and other firm activities. That leaves 62 waking hours of personal time for family, fitness, community, church, recreation, hobbies, commuting and other activities. How you spend the 10 hours a week (or whatever number) of investment time will ultimately determine the quality of your career. How you spend the 62 hours (or whatever number) of family and personal time will ultimately determine the quality of your life and family relationships.

In Rising Star, the protagonist Gina learns to balance her professional and personal life through coaching. How important is it for lawyers to maintain this balance, and what tips can you offer for achieving it?

I've coached many lawyers who are like Gina. I told them that in the legal profession there is no such thing as maintaining balance. One week a lawyer can be swamped with work and in another week the lawyer could be looking for work to do. Instead of focusing on balance I told lawyers to focus on their priorities, which always will include time for their family.

It Takes a Team addresses the issue of senior partners who may excel in client acquisition but struggle with team dynamics. What advice do you have for firms to cultivate a collaborative culture and address such challenges?

Going all the way back to class rank in law school, lawyers are focused on competing, not collaborating. Cultivating a collaborative culture is a challenge.

Here are some suggestions:

• Hire and train highly motivated lawyers with good people skills.

• In some way or another, reward collaboration, teamwork, and the lawyer's development of junior lawyers in the firm.

• Having written multiple books and given numerous presentations on career development, what do you believe is the most crucial piece of advice for young lawyers aiming to become successful rainmakers?

To me the most crucial piece of advice is to have a big enough "*why*" becoming a successful rainmaker is important to you that you will create plans: Five years, next year, next 90 days, next week and have the commitment and discipline to follow through.

PHOTO: Don Hughes, advocate for animal welfare, shares his inspiring journey from politics to fostering trust and compassion in rescue dogs.

From Policy to Paws

DON HUGHES
Navigating the World of Animal Rescue and Advocacy

BY Z. ROBERTS

Don Hughes, transitioning from politics to animal rescue, shares insights on fostering trust, overcoming challenges, and the transformative power of companionship.

Embarking on a journey from the intricacies of political science to the tender realm of animal rescue is not a conventional path, but for Don Hughes, it became an enriching odyssey. Graduating from the University of Illinois and later Harvard University, Don carved a distinguished career in state politics and public policy, particularly in healthcare and insurance. However, in 2017, the course of his life took a remarkable turn when he found his calling at the Maricopa County Animal Shelter in Phoenix, Arizona.

Living amidst the desert hues with his steadfast companion, Barbie, Don's story is one of profound transformation and unwavering dedication. His memoir, *The Mutt for Me,* delves into the intricate journey of nurturing Barbie, a rescue dog fraught with behavioral challenges. Through patience, understanding, and boundless compassion, Don navigated the complexities of earning Barbie's trust, unraveling layers of fear to reveal the resilient spirit within.

In an exclusive interview with Reader's House Magazine, Don sheds light on his motivations and experiences, offering invaluable insights into the world of animal rescue and the profound bond between humans and their four-legged companions. From the initial apprehension to the joyful moments of playfulness, Don's narrative resonates with the universal truth of resilience and the transformative power of companionship.

As Don recounts his journey, he encapsulates the essence of empathy and perseverance, urging others to embark on similar paths

The Mutt for Me by Don Hughes chronicles the heartwarming journey of nurturing Barbie, a rescue dog, amidst challenges and triumphs.

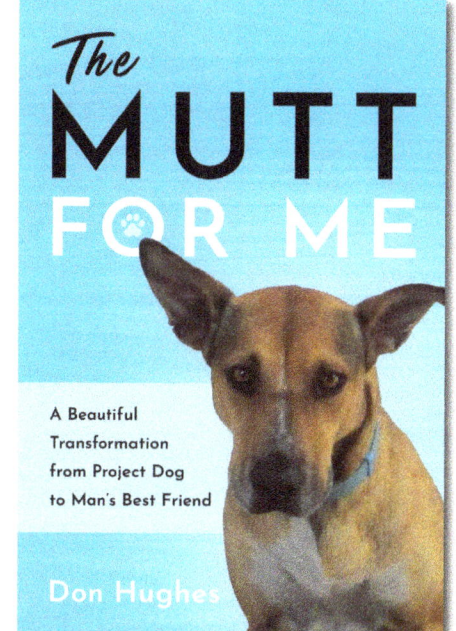

of compassion and advocacy for animals in need. Through his lens, the parallels between public policy and animal welfare become evident, highlighting the importance of communication, patience, and steadfast commitment in effecting positive change.

Join us as we delve into the heartwarming narrative of Don Hughes, a testament to the enduring bond between man and his faithful canine companion, and the profound impact of love, patience, and understanding in shaping lives, both human and animal alike.

Don, your journey from political campaigns to public policy and finally to volunteering at an animal shelter is quite remarkable. What inspired this shift in focus, particularly towards working with rescue animals?

In 2013, I began dating a woman who had five rescue dogs and ran a private shelter in Prescott, Arizona. Jenny opened my eyes to the world of animal rescue including the abuse we humans inflict on dogs and cats and just how terrific rescue dogs are. I began contributing financially to her rescue and others. I knew the money was needed and well spent; I began questioning whether just giving money was enough. If we want to make the world a better place, we have an obligation to give of ourselves and not just write a check.

Volunteering as an adoption counselor at our County Shelter, was the most rewarding and heartbreaking thing I've ever done. It would make me question my faith in humanity and restore it, often in the same day. While I can't change the world, finding a good home for a dog or cat, I can change their world.

Your memoir, The Mutt for Me, chronicles your experiences with Barbie, a behaviourally difficult rescue dog. Can you share a bit about the challenges you faced and the lessons you learned while helping Barbie overcome her fears and anxieties?

When I first met Barbie, she was afraid of everything, especially men. She had been brought in as a stray and had spent three months in the Shelter. The first time I met her, Barbie was curled up in a tight ball in the furthest corner of her kennel, hoping no one would notice her. When I looked into her eyes, there was no spark, no hope, just despair.

Barbie was afraid of men; the biggest challenge was simply gaining her trust. At first, Barbie did not want to be in the same room with me and would not eat or drink if I was in the kitchen. Through structure, walks and food, slowly, she began to trust me. The first slight tail wag at the door for our morning walk was a huge step forward.

Barbie had never been inside a house before, so house training was a big challenge. Before it didn't matter where she went, but now it did. Teaching her what I wanted from her was a major challenge for both of us. For every step forward, we seemed to take two steps back. Our communication improved, once I paid attention to bow, she was letting me know what she needed.

Adopting a rescue dog can be both rewarding and challenging. What advice would you give to others considering adopting a rescue animal, especially one with behavioural issues?

I would tell potential adopters not to expect the dog to be happy and playful the minute the dog enters your home. The Shelter is a scary place, going into a strange new environment is also scary. Be patient, remember the rule of 3. Three days for your new dog to decompress, three weeks before she learns your routine and three months before they finally settled in and feel comfortable in their new home.

Patience is key. There is a great dog hidden behind their fear just waiting to come out. All that behaviorally challenged dog needs is someone who's willing to try. The reward is well worth the hard work, the tears and sleepless nights.

Throughout your career in public policy, you've tackled various challenges in areas like health care and insurance. How do you see your experiences in policy shaping your approach to caring for animals and advocating for their well-being?

The communication skills needed to be effective in shaping public policy translate easily to caring and advocating for animals. Listening to what the adopter was looking for in a pet, asking the right questions, clearly explaining the dog's history and potential problems, ensuring that everyone in the family knew adopting a dog is a lifetime commitment. Not rushing the initial meeting.

These are basically the same steps in being an effective lobbyist or policy advocate.

Your memoir highlights the transformative power of the human-animal bond. Can you share a specific moment or experience with Barbie that particularly stands out to you as emblematic of this bond?

One night, I was working in my home office when I heard a commotion coming from the living room. When I went out to check on what was going on, I found Barbie was playing! She gave me her first play bow since she moved in. We played hide and seek; she loved finding me hiding in the bathroom or the laundry room. This was the first time in two months that Barbie played. She was finally learning to be a dog again. Seeing her transform from the scared dog who had given up on life to being so happy and playful made it all worthwhile.

> *Don Hughes embodies empathy, resilience, and unwavering dedication, illuminating the transformative bond between humans and their four-legged companions.*

Reader's House || 41

PHOTO: *Malcolm Welshman, celebrated veterinarian and author, sharing his incredible journey and love for animals*

From Vet to Bestselling Author
MALCOLM WELSHMAN

From London Zoo to Amazon's Bestseller List: Combining Veterinary Practice with Writing

BY DAN PETERS

Malcolm Welshman discusses his veterinary career, transition to bestselling author, and experiences as a cruise ship speaker, offering advice for aspiring writers.

Malcolm Welshman, a retired veterinarian and accomplished author, has led a life rich with remarkable experiences and fascinating encounters with animals. From his early days in Nigeria, where his passion for wildlife was ignited, to his tenure at London Zoo and his subsequent career in veterinary practice, Welshman's journey is as diverse as it is inspiring. His literary career took off with the publication of his debut novel, *Pets in a Pickle*, in 2011, which quickly became a bestseller on Amazon Kindle. This success paved the way for sequels like *Pets on Parad* and *Pets Aplenty*, charming readers with humorous and heart-warming tales.

In addition to his novels, Welshman is a prolific writer for national magazines and has contributed features to prominent publications such as the *Daily Mail* and the *Sunday Times*. His storytelling prowess extends to his memoir, *An Armful of Animals*, which recounts his unforgettable encounters with a variety of creatures. Welshman's vibrant narrative style brings to life the myriad of experiences he has had, whether they occurred in the wilds of Africa or the corridors of a veterinary hospital.

Welshman's career is not limited to writing; he is also a sought-after guest speaker on cruise ships, sharing his wealth of knowledge and amusing anecdotes with audiences around the world. His contributions to charity events, particularly those focused on animal welfare, further underscore his commitment to the field.

In this exclusive interview with *Reader's House Magazine*, Welshman delves into his extraordinary life, from his formative years in Africa to his current endeavours as an author and speaker. He discusses the pivotal moments that shaped his veterinary practice, the inspirations behind his beloved novels, and the evolution of his writing career. For aspiring writers, particularly those considering a later-in-life start, Welshman offers invaluable advice drawn from his own experiences. His journey is a testament to the rewards of perseverance and the joy of sharing one's passion through storytelling.

Your journey to becoming a vet took you from Nigeria to

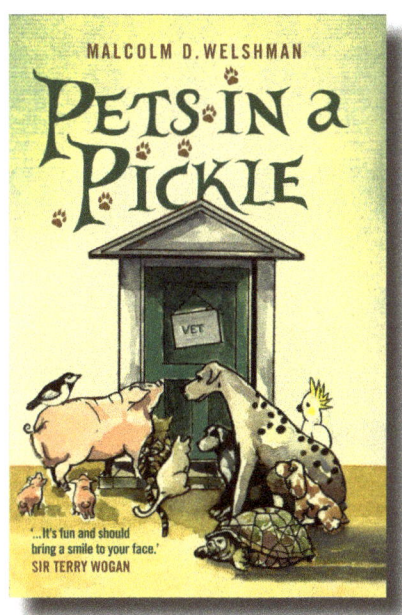

Malcolm Welshman's popular novels, including Pets in a Pickle, Pets on Parade, and Pets Aplenty, beloved by readers worldwide.

the UK, where you worked with a wide range of animals, including exotic species at London Zoo. How did these diverse experiences shape your approach to veterinary medicine, and how did they inspire your writing?

I've always been fascinated by the world of nature. When I was eight years old, my father, an army officer, was seconded to the Royal Nigerian Regiment and there followed four years in West Africa. Here, my interest in animals was further inspired by the exotic wildlife I encountered from parrots and monkeys to the occasional cobra and python. These experiences made me determined to become a vet and devote my life to caring and treating such animals. Once qualified, I spent time at London Zoo, honing my skills to treat any unusual creature likely to give a vicious bite or peck. Inspired by the likes of James Herriot and Gerald Durrell, I decided it worth attempting to share my experiences by writing about them. Hence, a writing career became established.

Your memoir, An Armful of Animals, promises to share fascinating encounters with creatures ranging from parrots to camels. Can you tell us about one particularly memorable animal encounter that left a lasting impression on you, either in your veterinary practice or during your travels?

Of all the animals I've encountered, one stands out in particular: Polly, our African Grey parrot. The vocabulary she acquired was astonishing - from 'Wakey, wakey rise and shine', army slang courtesy of my father, to 'You've got droopy drawers' via my mother - spoken in her tone of voice to prove it. Polly uttered the latter directly to the colonel's wife on an afternoon visit for tea, evoking blushes all round and a cackle of dirty laughter from Polly. When my father's tour of duty finished, Polly came back to the UK with us and resided in the kitchen of our new home. Imagine my concern when having just qualified as a vet, my mother phoned to say Polly was dying. She had a tumour on her neck which the local vet had said was inoperable. Rather than risk losing 13 years of wonderful companionship, I felt I had to attempt to remove the tumour myself. Which is what I did. Polly survived the operation. On the third day after it, she wobbled across her perch, put her head down for a scratch and in my voice,, albeit it croaky, said 'Wotcha mate'. I knew then she'd pull through. And pull through she did. Whenever I've had a challenging operation since, I only have to hear Polly's 'Wotcha mate' in my head, to help boost my confidence and strengthen the determination to succeed.

Your novels, such as Pets in a Pickle and Pets on Parade, blend humor and heartwarming stories centered around the experiences of a vet named Paul Mitchell. What inspired you to write fiction based on your experiences, and how do you balance the factual aspects of veterinary medicine with storytelling?

When I first started writing about veterinary matters it was along the lines of writing about what you know, in the form of animal- orientated features. As the years went by, more and more anecdotes emerged which eventually made me decide to put some together in a book. Rather than just describe my life story which has been the approach by many vets in the past, I felt a fictionalised backdrop would be easier and certainly provide a better framework on which to pin the animal encounters. Hence Paul Mitchell and the characters in Prospect House, the veterinary hospital. All are based on real characters and places, as are the clients though mixed and matched with the variety of animals encountered. This has made it easier to colour the characters and story lines and also ensure real people can't be identified. From the feedback from readers, it seems this approach works though on occasions I do feel I may have gone over the top with some of the more eccentric individuals I describe. Nicky Campbell, the BBC radio presenter, put it to me, that he found my witch, Madam Mountjoy, a totally unbelievable character. Lucky she didn't put a spell on him. But what the heck. Call it writer's licence.

In addition to your novels, you've contributed articles and stories to magazines like My Weekly. How does your background as a vet inform your writing for both fiction and non-fiction publications, and do you find one type of writing more challenging or rewarding than the other?

In my early days of trying to write something worthy of being published, I was very much into the realms of short stories especially of the twist-ending variety. Back then there was a magazine called Titbits which each week published such a story of around 600 words. I attempted to get one of my mine published in that magazine and did eventually succeed. At my fifteenth attempt. My second break was with a real life drama centred on a soldier ant attack on me when in Nigeria. It was then I realised real life stories stood a better chance of catching an editor's eye than fiction. And so it has proved. A Christmas true story about fattening up a goose to the editor of the national magazine, My Weekly, led to providing a monthly veterinary anecdotal page for the magazine and a question-and-answer column based on readers' letters sent in. That lasted 15 years. In more recent times, I've tended to seek out a current topic that has appeal, whether or not animal-orientated, and write a piece around that. It can be challenging as it often entails doing a bit more research to ensure the reader at least thinks you know what you're writing about. (I don't always.)

Your writing career gained momentum after you retired from veterinary practice, with your novels being republished and your experiences as a guest speaker on cruise ships. How has your perspective on writing evolved over the years, and what advice would you give to aspiring authors who are considering pursuing writing later in life?

The distractions (excuses) to getting 'pen on paper' are many. Coffee time. Walking the dog. It's a question of realising those distractions exist and finding ways to reduce if not entirely eradicate them. Always easier said than done. But done they must be. Or else that novel will always remain a dim and distant dream. To get going, start small. The likes of Anna Karenina might be your eventual objective, but a short feature in your local

PHOTO: *Robert Emmers, master storyteller and former investigator, brings his thrilling adventures to life through captivating fiction.*

The Unconventional Odyssey of
ROBERT EMMERS
A Journey Through Action, Mystery, and Imagination

BY DAN PETERS

Robert Emmers, from journalism to private investigation, now explores fiction. His stories blend action with existential themes, reflecting his diverse experiences.

Robert Emmers is a man of many stories, both lived and imagined. As a teenager, he dreamt of Paris and writing, but practicality steered him into a journalism career. The path was anything but dull. Emmers' professional journey took him through the gritty worlds of private investigation, insurance fraud detection, and crisis communications, each role offering a wealth of experiences that now fuel his fiction. Emmers' adventures range from evading federal subpoenas to being threatened by mob figures, from chasing fugitives to surveilling rogue priests.

Now residing in the serene woods of northwest Pennsylvania with his wife and dog, Emmers has returned to his original passion: writing fiction. His stories are imbued with the thrill of his past escapades and the disciplined, concise writing style honed in newsrooms. Emmers' latest work, *The Secret History,* and his captivating short story, *Where Did All the Dentists Go?* are testaments to his ability to weave action-packed narratives with existential undertones.

In this exclusive interview with Reader's House Magazine, Robert Emmers reflects on how his eclectic career has shaped his storytelling, explores the inspirations behind his dark and complex themes, and discusses his journey back to fiction. Join us as we delve into the mind of a writer who has lived the adventures most only read about, and now brings that same sense of excitement and discovery to his readers.

R. H. Emmers, your career has spanned journalism, insurance fraud investigation, crisis communications, and now fiction writing. How have these diverse professional experiences influenced your storytelling and writing style?

I'm a simple guy, so a simple answer: ala Papa Hemingway, as a newspaper reporter I learned to write cleanly and concisely. That carried over into my fiction writing. But it's not the whole truth. As an investigator, I came to love

Emmers' 'The Secret History' is a relentless rollercoaster of suspense and intrigue. With its gripping narrative and richly drawn characters, it's a must-read for fans of gritty thrillers.

Robert Emmers captivates with thrilling narratives, drawing from a life rich in adventure. His writing transcends boundaries, immersing readers in vivid, unconventional worlds.

action, chasing down a fugitive or fraudster and confronting him. And that has had an even greater influence on my writing of fiction: There's always action.

The Secret History delves into the world of government death squads, crime, and vengeance. What inspired you to explore such dark and complex themes in your fiction debut?

I once wrote a novel (which remains unpublished because it was total crap) featuring a character named Dahl who finds himself in situations inspired by my work in crisis communication: I was mostly a fixer, and mostly on the streets rather than writing talking points and so forth. One day I decided to resurrect Dahl in a short story; by accident, it grew and became a novel, The Secret History. It's set mainly in Mexico because I love Mexico. And some of the scenes in the novel are based on my own experiences as a fixer, but even more so by my imagination. But, as I say, it was an accident.

Where Did All the Dentists Go? presents a surreal and mysterious tale set in the village of M... What inspired the creation of this intriguing story, and what themes were you exploring through its narrative?

As with all my short stories, *Where Did All The Dentists Go* began when a first line magically appeared to me. At first, it was going to be an exploration of a weird relationship. Then one day I happened to read about johatsu, the Japanese phenomenon of people leaving their lives and disappearing. Viola, the story bloomed from there. I don't consciously worry about theme. But if there has to be an over-arching theme in my writing it's that you always keep moving, forward, backward, whatever, just don't let them catch you.

Your protagonist in Where Did All the Dentists Go? embarks on a journey of discovery in a seemingly ordinary yet enigmatic village. What parallels, if any, do you see between the protagonist's search for answers and your own journey as a writer returning to fiction writing?

My life has been an exploration. Probably that's why I've had so many different (and always fun) careers. The idea of exploration carries over into my fiction. Every character is looking for answers. For example, in The Secret History, all of the main characters are pretty despicable. But what makes them interesting to me is that they're all looking for answers, of one sort or another.

Throughout your writing, there's a sense of mystery and existential questioning. How do you balance crafting intricate plots with delving into deeper existential themes in your storytelling?

First, I prefer writing short stories rather than a novel. This is because I feel freer with the short story form, 5,000 words or so vs. 80,000 or more. One reason for this, I think, is the shortness itself: It'll be over soon, for good or bad, so don't worry about it and let the imagination roam. Just the thought of writing another novel makes me want to go back to bed. So, I'm working on a series of linked stories for my next book. But as to short stories: A line pops into my head and I write it down and that is the beginning of the story. Then the story goes where it wants to go, and the plot reveals itself. But in my experience a novel is different. It must be constructed bolt by bolt. So, I do write something of an outline beforehand laying out who does what to whom and so on: Everything has to connect. But that outline often goes out the window as characters take charge. As far as existential themes? I don't worry about themes in short stories; the story becomes what it wants to be. A novel is different, for me anyway. The theme I like best is seeking redemption and moving ahead.

Your writing often features unconventional settings and characters. What draws you to explore these unconventional elements, and how do you approach creating immersive and compelling fictional worlds for your readers?

I like writing about drunks, screw-ups, dopers and strange people caught in strange situations. Why? Probably because, even though I've had interesting jobs that involved plenty of interesting situations (I should tell you about the time my newspaper partner and I drove around one weekend with all our files dodging a federal subpoena) my life as a writer is pretty conventional: Wife, dog, house. So, of course, I like crooks and weirdoes. Am I compensating for my current life chained to a desk? Probably, but at least when I'm writing I can be a crook or a weirdo. The thing is, when I'm writing, if I'm really into it on any particular day, the world I'm writing about becomes real. So, yeah, I'm compensating.

Reader's House || 45

PHOTO: *Wayne English crafts riveting narratives, blending technical prowess with storytelling finesse, captivating readers with his diverse expertise.*

Exploring the Diverse Worlds of
WAYNE ENGLISH
A Journey Through Career, Creativity, and Crafting Compelling Narratives

BY DAN PETERS

Discover Wayne English's journey from engineering to writing, blending technical expertise with storytelling. Explore his novels, advice for writers, and upcoming series.

Wayne English's journey is a testament to the multifaceted nature of career paths in today's world. Residing in Coventry, Connecticut, alongside his wife, daughter, and Olive their yellow canary, Wayne has carved a remarkable niche that spans various disciplines. His professional odyssey encompasses roles as an Engineering Technician, Computer Scientist, Senior Technician, and educator, with stints in electric distribution, nuclear power, and Information Resources. Yet, it's his prowess as a writer that truly shines, boasting an impressive repertoire including five books and contributions to an array of local, national, and international publications, online and in print.

Intriguingly, Wayne seamlessly intertwines his occupational experiences with his passion for writing, resulting in narratives that are compelling and technically precise. Take, for instance, his short story *ShiftWorld*, where the protagonist's journey mirrors Wayne's own tenure in electric distribution and nuclear power, lending an authenticity that resonates with readers.

Wayne's literary endeavors span genres, from captivating historical fiction like *Attila's Revenge* to his upcoming series,*The Tory Town Chronicles,* set in a fictional town in Connecticut. In each venture, he deftly blends historical facts with fictional narratives, creating immersive worlds teeming with intrigue and emotion.

For aspiring writers embarking on their own publishing odyssey, Wayne offers sage advice rooted in his wealth of experience. He advocates for writing about topics one is professionally competent in, emphasizing the importance of thorough research and the dissemination of accurate information.

With a knack for making complex topics accessible, Wayne's writing reflects his passion for continual learning and his commitment to clarity. Whether unraveling the intricacies of web content optimization or demys-

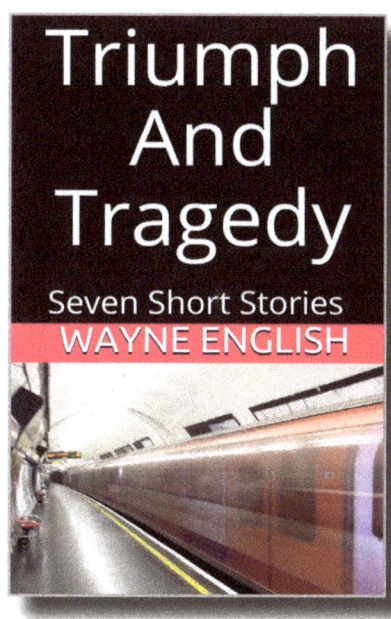

Triumph And Tragedy: Seven Short Stories - Wayne English's gripping collection explores the resilience of the human spirit through tales of adventure, perseverance, and unexpected twists. Now available on Kindle.

tifying social networking, Wayne's approachable style ensures that readers are both informed and engaged.

In essence, Wayne epitomizes the modern polymath, seamlessly traversing diverse domains with aplomb and leaving an indelible mark on each. As readers delve into his works, they are not just entertained but enlightened, invited on a journey where expertise meets imagination, and the boundaries of possibility are endlessly expanded.

Your career journey seems diverse, spanning from nuclear engineering to writing and publishing. How did you navigate these different fields, and what inspired your transition into writing?

Navigating Nuclear power, electrical distribution, and writing was not a problem. You see, I did not leave my full time job to write full time. I did both at the same time. As for inspiration, I enjoyed seeing my name in print and the more I wrote and published the more I enjoyed it. That has held over the years and continues to this day. I use my occupational experience to inform my writing. In my short story 'Shift World' the main character is assigned to work in an electric power station. The story is technically accurate from my twenty plus years working in electric distribution and nuclear power.

Attila's Revenge sounds like a captivating historical fiction. What drew you to Attila the Hun's story, and how did you approach blending historical fact with fictional narrative in your novel?

I saw Attila's Revenge as a story of love, hate, wealth, power. It's the ultimate in good versus evil. What drew me to the story was an article I read about how he died, which I found interesting, so I read more and more finally killing him, in the story, the way he actually died. That is, if the history as written is correct. We'll never know because his body has never been found.

Your upcoming series, The Tory Town Chronicles, is set in a fictional town in Connecticut, and sounds intriguing. Could you share a bit about the inspiration behind this series and what readers can expect from it?

I was inspired by wanting to write a contemporary series with wide latitude in characters, location, and plot. Readers can expect current and future technology wrapped up with a cast of characters and villains that is worldwide in scope. I do this by making the story about a heavy rigging crew that works worldwide providing oil field services and heavy rigging needs from building an experiment for a world class scientist to working on Alaska's North Slope. The characters are ex-military and civilian people of unquestioned competence.

As an experienced author, what advice would you give to aspiring writers who are just starting their journey in the world of publishing?

Write about material that you are professionally competent with. You've likely heard the saying, 'write what you know.' This is good and bad advice. It's good when your starting out and bad as your skills improve.

When you are able to take on work that require research, writing, editing, and maybe marketing as well. As to research, be careful when using the web as material there must be verified from at least two other trusted sources. Never - and I mean never - trust any one source online unless it's of unquestioned professional competence.

Your professional resume reflects a wealth of experience and expertise, from authoring books to training development and electric distribution.

How has your diverse background influenced your writing style and the topics you choose to explore in your books?

Much of my background finds its way into my work. This is true whether I'm writing fiction or nonfiction as I've used a great deal of technology so when writing about computers, social media, or writing content I've worked in those areas. A diverse background is an asset, but more important is solid knowledge, so you're capable of passing on solid, technically accurate, information and not just an uninformed opinion. When I worked in nuclear power many of the people who were anti-nuclear had no idea about the technology and I found myself responding to what people thought not what they knew. Those conversation were never pleasant as I found myself pitted against opinion, not facts.

You've written on a variety of topics, from web content optimization to social networking and job hunting using the web. What drives your interest in these diver-se subjects, and how do you approach making complex topics accessible to your readers?

I've always enjoyed learning new things, taking on new challenges, and have done many things besides writing such as: teaching photography, doing it professionally, and writing a monthly column for a magazine, working on a volunteer ambulance and running the training committee.

Making complex topics easy to understand is my forte. I believe that's from all the teaching I've done. When I worked in a photographic

department it was great fun. After the second or third explanation failed to explain something to a customer my creativity was tested to get the message across because no one is going to buy a camera they can't use. The same thing goes for writing. No one will read your material if they can't understand it. Unless, of course, you're writing a text book where students have access to people who can explain the material.

Reader's House || 47

PHOTO: *Jeff Kelland, an author and advocate, passionately explores societal issues through his multifaceted artistic talents.*

Championing Truth Through Fiction
JEFF KELLAND
Unveiling Injustice in Grace Ungiven

BY BEN ALAN

Jeff Kelland's Grace Ungiven confronts the Catholic clerical abuse crisis, blending fiction with raw truth to highlight power dynamics and survivors' resilience through meticulous character development and extensive research

Hailing from Newfoundland, Jeff Kelland embodies the essence of a multifaceted artist. As an independent author and publisher, he not only spins tales but also weaves intricate narratives that delve deep into the human psyche. His creative repertoire extends beyond the written word, encompassing a flair for music and visual arts. Yet, it's his unwavering commitment to shedding light on pressing societal issues that truly sets him apart.

Kelland's latest work, *Grace Ungiven*, stands as a testament to his dedication to confronting uncomfortable truths. Inspired by the harrowing revelations of the Catholic clerical child sexual abuse crisis, Kelland navigates the labyrinthine corridors of power and control within the Church with both empathy and unflinching honesty.

In a candid interview, Kelland shares the genesis of his novel, rooted in personal experiences and a year-long odyssey of research and reflection. Through meticulous character development, he breathes life into protagonists like Mickey Kavanaugh, whose quest for justice mirrors the resilience of abuse survivors grappling with profound trauma.

Grace Ungiven is not merely a story but a tapestry woven from the threads of original storytelling and stark reality. Kelland deftly balances the intricacies of narrative craft with the gravity of the issues he explores, creating a compelling tableau where intrigue, romance, and crime converge with themes of social justice and activism.

For Kelland, literature serves as a powerful conduit for fostering dialogue and catalyzing change. By melding elements of fiction with the stark truths of our world, he invites readers to confront uncomfortable realities with empathy and understanding.

As we delve into the pages of *Grace Ungiven*, we are reminded that the human experience is anything but monochromatic. Through Kelland's lens, we bear witness to the complexities of life, where shadows of darkness mingle with glimmers of hope, and where the pursuit of truth is intertwined with the quest for redemption.

In Jeff Kelland's literary universe, every word is a brushstroke, every page a canvas, and every story a beacon of illumination amidst the shadows.

Grace Ungiven by Jeff Kelland – a gripping narrative merging intrigue and social justice to confront the harsh realities of clerical abuse.

> Jeff Kelland masterfully intertwines narrative craft with social activism, creating compelling stories that illuminate profound truths and inspire change.

What inspired you to delve into the sensitive topic of the Catholic clerical child sexual abuse crisis for your novel Grace Ungiven?

Initially, it was the clerical sexual abuse scandal in the Roman Catholic Church and the coverup that continues to this day, as well as some personal experience I had with abuse as a boy. When the story first broke, I wrote a song in response, but this was not enough. As a non-Catholic, I was shocked to learn about the power and control the church held over followers' lives; even before considering the untold suffering and the dysfunction at issue. A year of research and 100+ interviews with everyday Catholics verified all this and more, and I felt compelled to share what I was learning.

Mickey Kavanaugh, the protagonist of Grace Ungiven, embarks on a quest for justice and redemption. How did you develop his character and the psychological impact of his experiences as an abuse survivor?

Almost all characters were generated by drawing from the amalgam of the thoughts, feelings, and experiences related to me in the interviews. Without using any of what I was told directly, they were all used to triangulate, as it were, to fill out the story and create plausible characters, including their thoughts and feelings. This informed the main character, Mickey, but also the characters that come to help him bring the priest to justice; helping Mickey brings them face to face with their own issues with the church, and the interviews proved to be an extensive resource for filling out these characters.

Grace Ungiven is described as a blend of original storytelling and raw truth. How did you navigate the balance between crafting a compelling narrative and addressing the serious real-world issues it explores?

My research strongly indicated that, for the most part, it is the many patriarchal ways that church leaders exercise so much power and control over the faithful that made the ongoing abuse scandal not only possible but inevitable, and I needed to create a story and set of characters that could get all this across to my readers. The interviews were invaluable in achieving this, but so was the ongoing scandal being revealed daily in the news. After all, it is by observing how these matters play out in reality that we find these serious real-world issues, and their incorporation into the narrative is key to the readers' enjoyment of the book and their appreciation of the real-world details the book reveals.

Given your extensive background in writing and community health, how do you see literature contributing to conversations about social justice and activism, particularly regarding issues like child abuse?

Writing and the arts in general are the places where our reality gains meaning, particularly things that the average person may not know or realize. They allow us to reveal what lies behind the facts and figures of this or that phenomenon in our world, and then to learn from it. Indeed, the arts have always been the best way to do this. And when the truth is especially hard to take, a well-researched and well-written book can sooth the reader, even as it informs and entertains.

In Grace Ungiven, you incorporate elements of intrigue, romance, and crime alongside the exploration of a serious social issue. How do these narrative elements enhance the reader's understanding and engagement with the story's central themes?

These elements are the nuts and bolts of our reality, and if an author hopes her/his book to be something readers will enjoy and appreciate, they must be shown in relation to the story and its subject matter. This achieves two things: it shows how the issue (s) is inextricably bound up with human life, and how it can be hidden in plain sight amid our everyday reality, which serves to justify the need for the book in terms of bringing awareness to the matter. Human life is anything but neat and tidy, and any book that purports to address a given subject in human life must reflect this.

PHOTO: *Anne Penn, true crime author and victims' advocate, in her study where she meticulously researches notorious criminal cases.*

Unmasking the Shadows
ANNE PENN
A Deep Dive into the Mind of a True Crime Author

Anne Penn has spent a lifetime immersed in the realm of true crime, driven by a relentless pursuit of justice for victims and their families. A multi-generational native of Sacramento, Penn's connection to the notorious East Area Rapist, who haunted her hometown, has fueled her mission to uncover the truth behind unsolved cases. Her five books on the Golden State Killer provide meticulously researched insights into crimes that have left an indelible mark on California's history.

With a robust background in psychology, criminal justice, and addiction studies, Anne Penn brings a unique perspective to her investigations. Her deep dive into the psyche of serial offenders, coupled with her personal experiences and connections to the cases she studies, offers readers an unparalleled view into the complexities of these heinous crimes. Penn's work is not just about chronicling events; it's about understanding the motivations behind them and seeking closure for those affected.

In her extensive career, Penn has delved into some of the most infamous criminal cases, including the Zodiac Killer and the Golden State Killer. Her dedication to uncovering the truth has led to significant revelations and has provided new avenues for law enforcement to pursue. Her commitment to victims' advocacy is evident in her efforts to bring cold cases back into the spotlight, pushing for DNA testing and continued investigation.

Anne Penn discusses her relentless investigation into the Golden State Killer and Zodiac Killer, blending psychology and forensics to advocate for victims and bring unsolved cases back into the spotlight.

Anne Penn's books are a testament to her unwavering resolve to ensure that justice is served. Her latest works, including *What If? Golden State Killer ZODIAC SOLVED* and *Serial Slaughter Zodiac Killer*, explore the possible connections between these notorious killers, presenting new evidence and challenging conventional narratives. Penn's meticulous research and compelling storytelling not only engage readers but also honor the victims and their families by keeping their stories alive.

In this interview, Anne Penn shares her journey, from her early fascination with true crime to her current projects aimed at solving decades-old mysteries. Her passion for justice, combined with her expertise in criminal psychology and forensics, makes her a formidable force in the true crime genre. Readers will find in Penn not just an author, but an advocate dedicated to shining a light on the darkest corners of criminal history.

Anne, your extensive background in sociology, addiction studies, psychology, criminal justice, and criminal law provides a unique perspective on the true crime genre. What inspired you to delve into writing about notorious cases like the Golden State Killer and the Zodiac Killer?

Your books not only explore the crimes themselves but also dive into the psychological and sociological factors behind serial offenders. How do you balance the portrayal of these complex individuals while honoring the victims

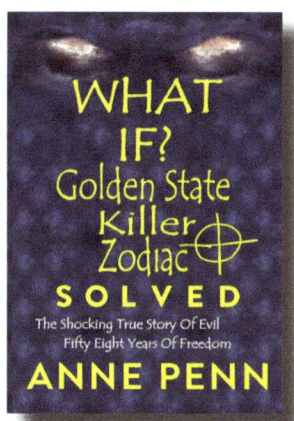
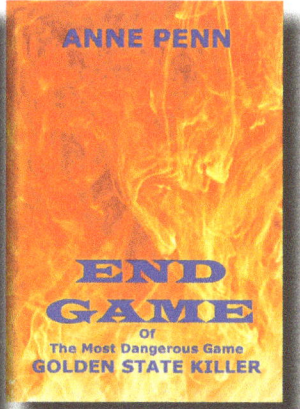

Anne Penn's compelling works on the Golden State Killer and Zodiac Killer, offering new insights and advocating for justice.

and their families?

At age 14 I was walking home. I was only two blocks away from safety when I was chased by two men in a truck and almost abducted. The fear I carried from then on was palpable. I realized I could have been taken never to be seen again. I got away by listening to my instincts. I grew up in Sacramento in the 1970's. There were many rapists, serial killers and others committing crimes all around the area. I had always had a fascination with true crime. The first murder I recall was of JFK. I was a child, but the impact was huge. The Zodiac and Manson murders I watched with fascination. Still a child, I tried to figure out how anyone could think they had the right to take someone's life from them and do so on purpose. My relatives worked in different areas of law enforcement and within the criminal justice system. One uncle actually was CHP in Solano county during the time of Zodiac. Later the Original Night Stalker killed my grandfather's son Lyman Smith and his wife Charlene in Ventura, CA. Like everyone for the next 38 years I wanted to

> Anne Penn's dedication to true crime is unparalleled, combining meticulous research with a profound empathy for victims and their families.

see the man who was doing such evil things caught. Amazingly the East Area Rapist, Original Night Stalker AKA Golden State Killer are one and the same man. It begged the question – was he also the Zodiac Killer?

Your books not only explore the crimes themselves but also dive into the psychological and sociological factors behind serial offenders. How do you balance the portrayal of these complex individuals while honoring the victims and their families?

I studied and sought to understand in depth how a serial offender is born. It was my thought as I tracked this serial killer that all of the psychological factors would help me figure out where he might still be (before his arrest). I grew up in this serial killers hunting grounds. I wanted this criminal caught. I was 20-22 when the East Area Rapist was active in my neck of the woods. My intention is to call attention to old cold cases of murder. That way I balance the portrayal of evil and still honor the victims especially by asking that the open cases be solved. I am an advocate for women first and foremost. I fight to get cases in front of DA Investigators and Law Enforcement asking them to test DNA, to solve what cases are still solvable because it matters.

Your books not only explore the crimes themselves but also dive into the psychological and sociological factors behind serial offenders. How do you balance the portrayal of these complex individuals while honoring the victims and their families?

My research process has been to look into historical records and newspaper articles that invariably tell one what exactly was going on in certain geographical locations during certain time frames. With great research one can see patterns, geographical areas of attack and actually see amounts of crime, close Mo's or even a tell or signature of an offender when they try to confuse Law Enforcement and others. They have a signature one can see even when they throw out red herrings and change what they do. An offender thinks they can confuse Law Enforcement by changing from bludgeon to stabbing to strangling. They think changing jurisdictions will confuse those who search for them. I always do my own research and avoid any outside influences or bias.

In Serial Slaughter Zodiac Killer, you offer new evidence and perspectives on the infamous crimes. What do you hope readers will take away from your exploration of these cases, particularly regarding the impact on the victims and their families?

In Serial Slaughter I present evidence, geographical profiles, MO's and more that tell of crimes that could not only be connected to the Zodiac Killer, but show that he continued to kill as he promised over time, murdering many women and girls. One of the things I hope readers will take away from reading Serial Slaughter is the knowledge that crimes are still solvable, that it is important to bring answers to families, and that crimes against women and girls matter. I present cold cases that can be solved because they have DNA to test. Two murders from this book were solved after I sent my book to DA Investigators.

Your dedication to bringing answers to families affected by violent crimes is evident in your work. How do you navigate the emotional challenges of delving into such dark subject matter while maintaining empathy for those involved?

I make sure to be aware of how I feel and if I need a break. There are times I can feel the effects of the deep dives into dark histories, but I know that someone needed to document these stories, someone needed to push those in power to solve these crimes even if they are 50 years old. They can do it and solving these crimes is important work. I never lose sight of why I do this work.

Looking ahead, do you have plans for future projects or cases you're eager to explore further? If so, can you provide any hints about what readers can expect next from you in the true crime genre?

My future plans include a book I am currently writing called Unsolved Cold Case Murder Files California. It will be complete August 2024. Also of interest I will write about a few solved crimes in National Parks in California. In addition, coming in June is my fictional analysis and homage to the character Dexter. I have been a huge fan of the series so I have written what I think while thanking all who created the characters for the Dexter series. Dexter fights for justice when the bad guys fall through the inevitable cracks of the criminal justice system.

An Intimate Memoir by
PENNY CHRISTIAN KNIGHT
Resilience: A Journey of Healing

Penny Christian Knight shares her journey of resilience, navigating trauma, and finding hope through her memoir trilogy, offering insights into healing and the power of self-expression.

BY BEN ALAN

Penny Christian Knight's life is a testament to the resilience of the human spirit. Having embarked on multiple careers, including modeling, acting, and working in various office roles, she eventually found her true calling as a social psychotherapist. However, it wasn't until her midlife return to academia at the age of 45 that she fully embraced her passion for psychology and English, earning degrees and accolades along the way.

Retiring from her private practice at the age of 89, Penny turned her attention to completing her autobiographical memoir trilogy, starting with DEVELOPING RESILIENCE: Secrets, Sex Abuse, and the Quest for Love and Inner Peace. But what motivated her to share such deeply personal experiences with the world?

In an exclusive interview with Reader's House Magazine, Penny candidly discusses her journey of self-discovery and healing. Reflecting on the emotional challenges of revisiting traumatic experiences, she shares how her journey toward resilience shaped her perspective on life.

"As I developed resilience, I found it helped me face many challenges that confronted me," Penny remarks. "Early on, I learned how to repress unpleasant memories... But it is essential to get in touch with our feelings, to name and express them to a trustworthy and safe person."

Throughout the interview, Penny emphasizes the importance of resilience in overcoming adversity and finding hope. She hopes that her memoir will inspire others to find courage and strength in their own struggles.

"I hope readers will learn that they can survive almost anything and that it helps to develop friendships with compassionate friends," Penny explains. "We must find and develop ourselves to become whatever we are meant to be and not run and hide."

As a seasoned social psychotherapist, Penny's insights into the healing process are invaluable. Drawing from her own experiences and professional expertise, she offers guidance on navigating trauma and finding catharsis through writing.

Her memoir not only serves as a testament to her own resilience but also as a source of inspiration for readers facing their own challenges. Through her candid storytelling and unwavering honesty, Penny Christian Knight reminds us that even in our darkest moments, there is always hope for healing and growth.

What motivated you to share your deeply personal story in Developing Resilience?

After writing an authentic personal essay during an Authentic Writing Workshop at Omega Institute of Holistic Studies in Rhinebeck, New York, I knew I had the beginning of a memoir, so I decided to return home and start one ten years ago at 80. I knew from then on that whatever I wrote would have to be authentic. I am a saver, having saved many letters, diaries, and journals where I acknowledged what happened to me, my reactions to whatever, and later, my healing journey.

Many named people in my story had passed, so I felt safe from their disapproval, allowing me to share it. I concluded that I had a mission to share my story to help others find hope, courage, and a means of growth to move forward with their lives and out of toxic situations that were holding them prisoner. One book grew to three, and I am currently editing the others.

How did you navigate the emotional challenges of revisiting traumatic experiences while writing your memoir?

For the most part, it was not difficult. By the time I reached 80 and beyond, my repressed memories had already appeared. Throughout my adult life, I obtained counseling and therapy many times to deal with the repressed outer layers as I reached inward to the core (like an onion). Having become a psychotherapist myself also helped me

> *Discover the transformative power of resilience in 'DEVELOPING RESILIENCE: Secrets, Sex Abuse, and the Quest for Love and Inner Peace,' Penny Christian Knight's compelling memoir trilogy.*

process the traumas before the creation of the books. Spiritually, I have also worked on forgiveness of my perpetrators.

Can you elaborate on the role of resilience in your journey, and how it has shaped your perspective on life?

As I developed resilience, I found it helped me face many challenges that confronted me. Early on, I learned how to repress unpleasant memories by saying, "It doesn't really matter." That was effective. I also learned that I needed to keep busy and involved in activities that usually kept me safe and connected to others. I continued doing that later in life when the challenges were even more significant. I learned other things that kept me engaged with study or personal growth. The distractions worked to keep material repressed until I reached a point in my life where I began developing wisdom and understanding. I left out one crucial detail. It is essential to get in touch with our feelings, to name and express them to a trustworthy and safe person, such as a therapist who wasn't available to me when young.

What message or lessons do you hope readers will take away from your book?

I hope readers will learn that they can survive almost anything and that it helps to develop friendships with compassionate friends. We survivors go on despite what happens to us. We must find and develop ourselves to become whatever we are meant to be and not run and hide. There are many different agencies from which we can get help today or through the help of a therapist.

I found that writing about these things really helped me. We can write to the person who harmed us and tell them off but not send the letter. This is highly therapeutic. The idea is to get the trauma outside of ourselves so it isn't harming us internally. I have chronic pain from holding on to my repressed material for too long.

How did your experiences as a social psychotherapist influence the narrative and themes of your memoir?

My experiences did not influence the recorded material from diaries and letters. However, my experiences did in many of my comments and asides throughout the books. I commented about my naivete or things I might have done differently. Readers with similar backgrounds of trauma or marital difficulty can benefit from those comments.

My experience as a therapist was immensely helpful in how I created the books. The knowledge I have gained from my training and experience has helped me look for things others might not be aware of.

Were there any moments during the writing process that were particularly cathartic or healing for you?

Particularly cathartic and healing moments included the entire section on my marriage and divorce from my husband. The more I edited, read, and reread that material, I found myself becoming angrier and angrier. I don't recall that I was close to feeling that angry at the time when I should have been. It might have given me the energy or strength to leave that situation earlier. However, I was engaged in counseling at the time, which dissipated the anger which I experienced as anxiety.

PHOTO: Penny Christian Knight, retired social psychotherapist and author, shares her journey of resilience and healing through her autobiographical memoir trilogy

PHOTO: Wendy Zuccarello, author extraordinaire, infuses her stories with warmth, authenticity, and a touch of magic.

Crafting Love Stories with
WENDY ZUCCARELLO
From Animal Science to Romance Novels - Exploring the Journey of a Unique Voice in Literature

BY ANNA HARLOWE

Discover Wendy Zuccarello's journey from veterinary science to crafting heartfelt romances. Themes of love, forgiveness, and diversity shape her novels, resonating with readers worldwide.

Wendy Zuccarello, a remarkable voice in contemporary romance and romantic suspense, is more than just an author. With a background as eclectic as her storytelling, she weaves tales that resonate with readers far beyond the confines of a traditional romance novel. Wendy's journey into the world of literature began later in life, after dedicating two decades to the veterinary industry, where she tended to creatures ranging from hamsters to hippos. Her experiences have left her with more than just scars—they've given her a profound understanding of life's complexities, which she masterfully channels into her writing.

In her interview with Reader's House Magazine, Wendy sheds light on the driving forces behind her storytelling. Themes of love, forgiveness, and personal growth are not just tropes for her; they are integral elements that shape her characters' journeys. Her belief in the significance of the path to a happy ending is evident in her work, where she delves deep into the challenges and triumphs that pave the way for true love.

What sets Wendy apart is her unique perspective, stemming from her background in animal science and veterinary technology. Animals aren't just props in her stories; they are essential characters, each with their own role to play in the romance unfolding on the pages. From African Penguins to chipmunks, Wendy infuses her narratives with the warmth and authenticity drawn from her firsthand experiences.

Loudening Silence, Wendy's poignant exploration of deaf representation, is a testament to her commitment to inclusivity. Inspired by her own children's journey with

Enter worlds of love, forgiveness, and second chances with Wendy Zuccarello's captivating novels. Which story will capture your heart next?

hearing impairment, the novel is a heartfelt tribute to their resilience and strength. Wendy's dedication to accurate portrayal shines through, thanks to meticulous research and personal anecdotes woven into the fabric of the story.

The Healing Mountain Series, Wendy's debut work, delves into the complexities of forgiveness and redemption. Rooted in her own experiences, these stories resonate on a deeply personal level, offering readers a glimpse into the transformative power of forgiveness. Maine, with its breathtaking landscapes and serene beauty, serves as a fitting backdrop for these tales of love and healing.

As a self-published author, Wendy's journey has been both challenging and rewarding. The satisfaction of holding her own book in her hands is unparalleled, but it comes with a price—complete control and responsibility. Yet, Wendy's advice to aspiring authors remains steadfast: never give up, write from the heart, and embrace the journey, regardless of the obstacles.

With Wendy Zuccarello at the helm, romance literature isn't just about fairy tale endings—it's about navigating the twists and turns of life, finding love in unexpected places, and embracing the beauty of second chances. So, dive into her world, where love is real, forgiveness is transformative, and happily ever afters are earned, one page at a time.

> Wendy Zuccarello's narratives blend realism with romance, fostering empathy and celebrating the resilience of the human spirit.

Your novels explore themes of love, forgiveness, and personal growth. What draws you to these themes, and how do they influence your storytelling?

Relationships are not always easy, and there are so many things in life that can impact them. I have always wanted to reflect this in my writing. Happily ever afters are amazing, but the journey there is often filled with bumps, unexpected turns, and immense challenges. There is so much more to the classic "boy meets girl; boy and girl fall in love; boy and girl live happily ever after," and that is what I write. The journey is by far just as important as the outcome. My writing is heavily influenced by personal experience, and I strive to tell stories that are real.

Your background in animal science and veterinary technology is quite unique for a romance author. How does your past experience inform your writing, if at all?

I absolutely love including animals in my books. They have such an important role in the lives of so many people that they deserve to play their part in the romance world. One of my favorite books that I wrote, Never Let Go, includes some aspects of one of my previous jobs. The main character, Lia, is a penguin keeper at an aquarium. Some of my favorite memories of working with African Penguins are included in that book – all true stories. I also include dogs in several of my books, and even a chipmunk, based on Munchkin, the chipmunk that I hand feed in my back yard.

Loudening Silence features a protagonist who is deaf, adding diversity and representation to your story. What inspired you to incorporate deaf representation, and what research did you undertake to ensure accurate portrayal?

This story has been a long time coming for me. When I began graduate school, I wanted my thesis novel to be something meaningful, and Loudening Silence was born. Both of my teenagers are hearing impaired. Their diagnoses as toddlers were extremely difficult to come by, and more than challenging to understand as a parent. It was a terribly long road, but both handled it with overwhelming strength and positivity. I have watched them struggle and overcome so much in their short lives and wanted to use that inspiration the best way I could. The book is dedicated to my kids, Kaitlyn and AJ. The amazing story of Kaitlyn getting her hearing aids for the first time is there as well.

The Healing Mountain Series delves into the complexities of relationships and the journey towards forgiveness. Can you discuss the significance of forgiveness in your series and why it's a central theme?

This series is special to me not only because they were the first I published, but because parts of the stories are based on personal experience. Forgiveness is a difficult concept in so many situations. It is about finding peace and inner strength. It can allow you to heal, to grow, and move on, but you must be willing to let it in. These books were written with the hopes of sending the message that it is okay to struggle, but it is important not to let it hold you back. These characters will always hold a special place in my heart as they helped me find my writing voice and gave me the strength to put my heart on paper.

Maine serves as a backdrop for some of your novels. What significance does this setting hold for you personally, and how does it influence the stories you tell?

I love Maine. I went there for the first time in high school, and it took root in my heart. The beauty, the peace, the simplicity… there is nothing like it. When I began writing Finding an Anchor, there was no question in my mind about the setting. A few years ago, I took my daughter to Acadia National Park for a long weekend, and it is something I will never forget. To be able to share something so special with her means the world to me.

I am having trouble letting go of the characters from The Healing Mountains Series so I'm sure they will pop up again soon. They seem to have a lot more to say and I think I may have to continue their stories.

As a self-published author, what has been the most rewarding aspect of your writing journey, and what advice would you offer to aspiring authors looking to self-publish their work?

There are no words to describe holding a book that you wrote in your hands. Each and every time I open that box, there are tears and an immense sense of satisfaction and relief. Being a self-published author is amazing because you have complete control of your work. But you must remember that you have complete control of your work. Editing, formatting, design, story, publication, promotion, etc… it's all on you. It is a lot of work, but it is more than worth it.

My advice is and will always be, never give up. Write what you love. Give it your all. Don't look back.

And the most important thing is that as an indie-author, your sales DO NOT define your success.

PHOTO: *Carina Steinbakk's 'Flames of Eader' captivates with its blend of magic and science, weaving a tale of resilience and heroism.*

Unveiling the Magic
CARINA STEINBAKK
Exploring the Intersection of Magic and Science
Crafting Heroes in the Battle Between Light and Darkness

BY Z. ROBERTS

Carina Steinbakk, a Norwegian author renowned for her debut novel *Flames of Eader*, beckons readers into a realm where magic intertwines with science and where heroes navigate the intricate dance between light and darkness. In this urban fantasy, Steinbakk masterfully constructs a narrative brimming with energy imbalances resonant with our contemporary world. Her prose is a tapestry woven with vibrant descriptions, compelling characters, and plots that quicken the pulse.

Carina Steinbakk discusses her inspiration from merging magic and science, influences from her Norwegian upbringing, and themes of resilience in 'Flames of Eader.'

As an author deeply rooted in both the mystical and the pragmatic, Steinbakk's inspiration for *Flames of Eader* springs from the convergence of these seemingly disparate realms. For her, magic and science are not mutually exclusive but rather threads in the same cosmic fabric, waiting to be unraveled. Through characters like Grey, the protagonist, she explores the nuanced layers of humanity, where bravery coexists with doubt, and where kindness holds as much power as any spell.

Steinbakk's nomadic upbringing, traversing landscapes from the fjords of Norway to the moors of Scotland, infuses her world-building with a rich tapestry of Norse mythology and Scottish legends. These experiences, coupled with her background in renewable energy development and tech entrepreneurship, imbue her storytelling with authenticity and depth. Readers will find echoes of her own voice in Grey's wit, sarcasm, and indomitable spirit—a spirit shaped by real-world challenges and triumphs.

Within the pages of *Flames of Eader*, Steinbakk delves into themes of trust, resilience, and unexpected alliances. Through Grey's journey, readers are invited to ponder the intricacies of forging

Flames of Eader by Carina Steinbakk invites readers on a journey where magic collides with science and heroes navigate the labyrinth of light and darkness.

new bonds, confronting past traumas, and finding strength in the face of adversity. As the battle between light and darkness unfolds, Steinbakk's narrative serves as a beacon, illuminating the path toward balance and resilience in a world fraught with chaos.

Ultimately, Steinbakk's hope is that readers will not only be entertained by the tale of *Flames of Eader* but also find a renewed sense of wonder in the magic that surrounds them. Through her storytelling, she invites us to discover the magic within ourselves, to embrace the energy that flows through our lives, and to craft our own destinies amidst the tumult of existence.

What inspired you to merge

Carina Steinbakk, author of 'Flames of Eader, delves into the enchanting world of urban fantasy in this exclusive interview.

elements of magic, science, and strong heroes in your fantasy novel, Flames of Eader?

As my background is founded in both believing in the magic in the world as well as the pragmatism that comes with our scientific foundations, Flames of Eader evolved as an intersection of these two beliefs. Someone once said that magic is simply science that we do not yet understand, and this is reflected in the story of Grey and Eader. From the hidden world of Eader, where there are natural powers, magical creatures and ancient energies protecting, and threatening Earth, to the simple magic of a library, it all finds a place in Flames of Eader. When it comes to the character development, it was important to me that they as complicated, yet simple as we all are. In my mind, being honest and kind is as much a superpower as being able to shoot lasers from your eyes, and having doubts while being brave is a normal balance with even the strongest hero. Grey, our protagonist, is a nerd, a geek and a lover of all things fantasy when he gets dragged into the world of Eader, and learns about his own strengths and weaknesses. We get to learn about his past and how he handles the challenges thrown at him, all with the sarcasm, wit and brains you can expect from a millennial.

Can you share how your Norwegian upbringing and experiences living in Scotland influenced the world-building and mythology in your book?

I grew up as a bit of a nomad, and therefore I had the opportunity to experience new places and I relished getting lost in my new neighbourhoods in Norway, as well as envisioning where I might bump into a mountain troll or a holder, discovering the quiet nooks of Glasgow, the gloomy alleys of Aberdeen, and the moors of the Scottish highland —all of which became wellsprings of inspiration for my writing with the Norse mythology, and intriguing legends of Scotland.

As someone with a background in renewable energy development and tech entrepreneurship, how do these real-world interests intersect with your storytelling in Flames of Eader?

Anyone who knows me will recognise my 'voice' in my writing. Even in the way Grey talks and behaves, in how he sees a challenge as a way to find a positive outcome, or to explain the science in our every day lives. He might be little bit of a sarcastic know-it-all, but hey, where is the fun in life without a little sarcasm?

Could you delve into Grey O'Shearan's character arc and what makes him a compelling protagonist in the battle between light and darkness?

Grey has had a rough start in life, which has shaped his view on life and other people, making him a bit of a hermit. As he gets more insights into his former life, where he came from and his own abilities, he grows as both a man, friend and hero. He never lost his sense of humour, though we do get to experience how it goes from being a survival technique to more of a crutch in dealing with battles and new relationships. His insights into technology, fantasy books and engineering experience gives him specific tools to support his abilities, and to trust in the way forward.

In Flames of Eader, you explore themes of trust and unexpected alliances. How do these themes play out in Grey's journey and his interactions with the inhabitants of Eader?

As Grey has had a poor experience with people in general throughout his young life, it takes him some time to warm up to and understand his new reality. This especially shows when dealing with Callen, his former best friend and sparring partner, as well as Darby, a fellow Fior and the one who could have shone some light on his past much earlier. We see Grey struggle with adapting to his new role, especially when he realises the people of Eader has special ties to him and his past. Forging new bonds from old memories and learning who you can trust becomes a centrepiece in the story.

What do you hope readers will take away from the message or themes of balance and resilience presented in your novel?

In my heart I fiercely believe that magic is around us everywhere, and all we need to do is to learn to look for it. This is what I hope readers will take from the story. Especially in the types of energies we surround us with, that we can choose to do with the energy available to us as we wish and with this, we can create our own magic.

Journey of Resilience
BETH JORDAN

Exploring Cultural Identity, Grief, and Self-Discovery in 'Thank You for the Kiss'

Beth Jordan shares her diverse life experiences and their influence on her debut novel, Thank You for the Kiss, set in Cuba, delving into themes of resilience and personal transformation.

BY Z. ROBERTS

In the tapestry of life, some threads weave stories of remarkable diversity, resilience, and profound self-discovery. Beth Jordan's journey is a testament to this rich narrative tapestry, as she generously shares her odyssey of cultural exploration, personal growth, and creative expression in her debut novel, *Thank You for the Kiss*.

Beth's narrative begins in the vibrant hues of India, where storytelling and heritage were ingrained in her upbringing. From these roots, her path meandered across continents, from the corridors of a Convent school in the UK to the bustling streets of entrepreneurial ventures. Each chapter of her life, whether as a nurse, a teacher, or an anthropologist, served as a canvas for empathy, observation, and the intricate weaving of human stories.

Thank You for the Kiss unfolds against the backdrop of Cuba, a land both enchanting and perilous, where Beth found solace and inspiration amidst personal loss and profound cultural encounters. Through the eyes of her protagonist, Gina, readers embark on a journey of resilience, navigating the complexities of grief, identity, and the allure of a foreign land.

Drawing from her deep well of anthropological insight and global curiosity, Beth breathes life into Cuba's landscape and its people, capturing both the vibrant spirit and the haunting shadows that linger beneath the surface. Through Gina's transformative journey, Beth invites readers to contemplate the resilience of the human spirit, the power of inner strength, and the gentle reminder to tread with compassion in times of adversity.

As Beth's narrative unfolds, it becomes clear that *Thank You for the Kiss* is more than a memoir—it is a testament to the universal human experience, where loss and hope intertwine, and where the echoes of one's journey resonate across cultures and continents. It is a story that beckons readers to listen, to empathize, and to discover the beauty that emerges from life's most profound moments of challenge and triumph.

Your background is incredibly diverse, spanning from nursing and teaching to entrepreneurship and writing. How have these varied experiences influenced your approach to storytelling, particularly in your debut novel, *Thank You for the Kiss*?

Each of my careers was people centric, forming strong bonds through empathy and observation of cultural similarities

Dive into the pages of 'Thank You for the Kiss' as Beth Jordan's debut novel unfolds against the backdrop of Cuba's vibrant landscape.

Beth Jordan, author of 'Thank You for the Kiss,' reflects on her journey of cultural exploration and personal growth.

and differences in order to work in new environments and better understand their needs and what I needed for my own work. I listened to their stories and in my head wove them into my own life, which became its own unique story.

Thank You for the Kiss explores themes of cultural identity, grief, and self-discovery against the backdrop of Cuba. What drew you to set your novel in Cuba, and how did you incorporate your own experiences and observations into the narrative?

In 2014/15, I visited Cuba on holiday, a new part of the world to explore and a new culture. After a painful separation of 23 years and my mother's death in 2011, I needed to find a new life reference to overcome my deep loss of two of the most important people in my life. I fell in love with Cuba the island, its similarity to my childhood life in India, its own grief and resilience and its 'forever' hope. The people I met, the dark experiences that emerged creating a dantesque inferno, became the backdrop to my first novel.**Gina, the protagonist of your novel, undergoes a journey of personal transformation throughout the story. Can you discuss the inspiration behind her character and the challenges she faces as she navigates through grief and deception in a foreign land?**

This memoir is based on the author's own life events in Cuba, her adventuress soul and constant curiosity becoming her nemesis. Her underlying grief altered her usual decision making process. Cuba's political impact on its people touched her heart but misled her into believing she could be a force for good. She succumbs to the locals' need to escape and flee their trapped lives, entrapping herself. But her old warrior self surfaces as she determines to recover her loss of self worth and financial investments. Her own cultural beliefs strengthen her resolve.

Your bio mentions a deep interest in anthropology and a passion for exploring global cultures. How did your studies in anthropology inform your writing process, particularly in capturing the cultural nuances and complexities depicted in your novel?

Studying anthropology allowed me to see beyond the palm trees and white beaches, beyond tourism and the glamour of exotic poster places. Undersanding in general cultural nuances I was able to quickly empathise with the people, their lives, listen to their stories, music and traditions (the pig feast) which vividly allowed me to describe in detail and colour all that I saw.

Thank You for the Kiss delves into the concept of resilience and the struggle to rebuild one's life after profound loss. What message or insight do you hope readers take away from Gina's journey, especially in terms of overcoming adversity and finding inner strength?

Never make decisions of importance when in a state of grief, but if you do remember to be gentle with your self, remember what your original intention was, remember the culture into which you stepped into. What had you wanted to contribute to it, did all gain from it?

The setting of Cuba is portrayed as both enchanting and perilous in your novel. Can you discuss your approach to depicting Cuba's landscape and its people, balancing the allure of the country with the darker aspects of Gina's experience?

I wanted to paint Cuba as a background of hope and inspiration, through its peoples' vibrant sense of pride, trapped in a time warp and desperate for change, with always a sense of darkness still shackling them to an old man's dream. Gina's unexpected experiences wove themselves on top of this tapestry, mirroring and matching what she experienced. Their outcomes inextricably bound.

Reader's House || 59

The Art of Storytelling
BOBBI GROOVER
Exploring History, Humanity, and the Heart through the Eyes of a Literary Artisan

Bobbi Groover discusses character depth, historical accuracy, equine influences, and the emotional tapestry of her narratives in this captivating interview.

BY A. HARLOWE

Bobbi Groover is a literary artisan whose tapestry of tales weaves together the threads of history, humanity, and the heart. Her upbringing, shaped by the serene landscapes of rural life, imbued her stories with the essence of authenticity, drawing readers into worlds both familiar and fantastical.

In an exclusive interview with Reader's House Magazine, Groover delves into the depths of her creative process, offering insights into the intricate dance between character development and the exploration of human emotions. For Groover, understanding her characters is paramount, akin to knowing the rhythm of her own heartbeat. It's this intimate acquaintance that guides her pen, steering the narrative through the twists and turns of their emotional landscapes.

Her narratives are often a journey through time, as historical settings serve as the backdrop for her vivid characters to inhabit. Groover's meticulous research breathes life into bygone eras, ensuring that every detail resonates with historical accuracy while remaining compelling and engaging.

Yet, it's not just humans who populate Groover's worlds; her affinity for equines adds another layer of depth to her storytelling. Horses, as integral characters, mirror the emotions and struggles of their human counterparts, creating a symphony of emotions that resonates with readers in profound ways.

From the complexities of loyalty and deception to the tender embrace of love, Groover's narratives explore the depths of the human experience. Each story is a tapestry carefully woven, its threads drawn from the fabric of history and the complexities of human nature.

As she embarks on her latest endeavor, *TruDeceit*, Groover once again invites readers on a journey through time, this time to post-Gold Rush America. Against the backdrop of historical events, her characters grapple with vengeance, love, and redemption, their arcs shaped by the tumultuous currents of history.

In the realm of literature, Bobbi Groover stands as a luminary, illuminating the human condition with her storytelling prowess. Through her words, she invites readers to embark on a journey of discovery, where history and humanity intertwine, leaving an indelible mark on the soul.

Given your background in psychology and English, how do you approach character development and the intricacies of human emotions in your writing process.?

I never start my writing until I know my characters as well as I know myself. For me it feels more

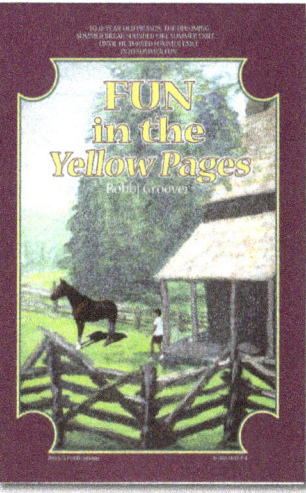

Bobbi Groover's novels: Where history unfolds, characters breathe, and emotions run deep, inviting readers on unforgettable journeys of discovery.

important than an outline of the story. I always have a general idea of where the story is headed. Because human emotions are so intricate, if one of the characters veers off course, knowing what's in their head and their heart will decide if the tangent remains.

Your stories often intertwine historical settings with vivid characters. What draws you to these particular periods in history, and how do you ensure historical accuracy while still crafting engaging narratives?

While investigating my family genealogy, I found many engaging stories within my own family during the American 1800's. To check for accuracy I drove many of the routes of my stories, visiting cemeteries and county courthouses. To my surprise I found distant elderly relatives, delighting in their stories of long ago times. I explored their homes from a turbulent era with the secret passageways and 'peep' holes. My discovery was literally a treasure trove of ideas and narratives. I felt as if I had already lived my stories and simply had to write them down.

Your experience as a third-generation equestrian seems to influence your writing, particularly in the incorporation of equine characters. How do you balance the portrayal of animals alongside human characters, and what unique challenges or joys does this bring to your storytelling?

Horses have been part of my makeup as far back as I can remember. Equines are named characters in my stories and often play important roles in the plot. How my human characters respect and care for their horses gives the reader a glimpse into their personalities as well as their view of other living, breathing creatures. A fourteen hundred pound animal can also create situations where a human might do something completely 'out of character' without shocking the reader while divulging important issues. The antics and feelings of the equines (yes, horses express a complex range of feelings if one chooses to listen) can wring emotions from the human characters in quite unique ways that might otherwise be challenging.

Inside the Grey explores themes of loyalty, deception, and love amidst the backdrop of conflict. Can you share how you navigate weaving complex plots while maintaining the emotional depth of your characters?

Alright, I'll confess to a bit of madness. Before putting pen to paper, I search the public domain for pictures of what my characters look like in my head. I then frame those pictures and pass them frequently on my daily routine. Being greeted by name each time I pass, the personalities behind those pictures soon become familiar friends and eventually that makes them real, as real as flesh and blood. Once I understand these individuals in depth, their best and their worst, the rest flows easily. No matter how complex the tapestry of the plot, the hero and heroine make their thoughts and emotions known in my head. Sometimes at night I awaken to find them gabbing that they don't like the way I've portrayed them in a certain scene. 'They' insist on it being changed to their liking, to wring out every emotion. I grab paper and record what they are saying and feeling. Needless to say, when the story ends and their pictures are retired to the walls of my studio, I am lonely for their constant companionship…at least until the next story begins.

Fun in the Yellow Pages appears to blend elements of juvenile fiction with themes of growth and self-discovery. What inspired you to write for a younger audience, and how do you approach crafting narratives that resonate with both children and adults?

My juvenile title was aimed at the theme of growth and self-discovery. I had worked with a troubled youth as well as an abused horse. The story tumbled out that perhaps the two might help each other. I interviewed the teenage son of a good friend to keep me on track and 'inside the head' of a fifteen-year-old so the narrative would ring true with my intended readers.

In your upcoming work TruDeceit, you delve into a tale of vengeance, love, and redemption set against the backdrop of post-Gold Rush America. Could you discuss how historical events influence your storytelling and shape the arcs of your characters?

In *TruDeceit* Rafe Buchanan returns home from the gold fields, an event which changes the course of his life. He spends the next sixteen years searching for answers for his grief. Though a major in the Civil War, he prays for death in every battle. Events completely out of his control change his life's course again and again. Unbeknownst to him, the bloody battle of Gettysburg which nearly ends his life, turns out to be the main event that saves him in every way. I use the historical events of the times to challenge my characters to secure their ultimate goal. The story told is…when things are out of their control, does it bring out the best or the worst in them?

> Bobbi Groover's storytelling prowess intricately weaves together history, humanity, and heart, leaving an indelible mark on readers' souls.

Available in
PRINT

Americas to Australia Europe to Africa Reader's House is available over 190 countries and thousands of retaiers, platforms including Amazon, Barnes & Noble, Walmart, Waterstone's .....

ELECTRONIC

It is an electronic (flip book) format and interactive. Accessable from electronic devices like pc, smart phone, notepads..

ONLINE

All interviews, we conduct make them accessable online for free.

SOCIAL MEDIA

We are on Facebook, Instagram and X. Please follow us on social media @readershousemag

contact us today for an interview opportunity at
editor@readershouse.co.uk

YES! I would like a subscription to

☐ Current Issue for ☐ Includes Shipping and Handling
☐ One-Year Subscription (_____ Issues) for
☐ Two-Year Subscription (_____ Issues) for

☐ I am a renewing a current subscription   ☐ I am a new subscriber

Name: _____   Phone: _____
Shipping Address: _____
Billing Address: _____
Email: _____

☐ Yes, I would like to receive updates, newsletters and special offers
☐ No, I would NOT like to receive updates, newsletters and special offers

Payment Type: ☐ Cash   ☐ Check

Subscribe Now!

Please mail this form to:
Magazine Name: *Reader's House* by Newyox 200 Suite, 134-146 Curtain Road EC2A 3AR London   readershouse.co.uk

www.ingramcontent.com/pod-product-compliance
Lightning Source LLC
Chambersburg PA
CBHW040315100526
44585CB00028BA/2960